THE FAKERS

The Fakers

Exploding the Myths of the Supernatural

Danny Korem
and Paul Meier, M.D.

Distributed by
BAKER BOOK HOUSE
Grand Rapids, Michigan

Library of Congress Cataloging in Publication Data

Korem, Danny.
    The fakers.

    Includes bibliographical references.
      1. Psychical research—Controversial literature.
2. Occult sciences—Controversial literature.
3. Christianity and psychical research. 4. Christianity and occult sciences. I. Meier, Paul D., joint author. II. Title.
BF1042.K67   133.8   80-23180
ISBN 0-8007-1130-0

We dedicate this book to Mark Lundeen for his invaluable assistance and tenacious pursuit of the truth.

Contents

Foreword   9

Introduction   11

1 A Lesson in Deception   15

2 A Twitch Is the Snitch   38

3 The Pendulum—Belief Suspended   45

4 The Dowsers Take a Dunking   52

5 Table Tilting Set on an Even Keel   60

6 The Ouija Board—Spelling in Motion   67

7 Automatic Writing   73

8 Psychic Surgery: The Hands Are Quicker Than the Blade—Or a Cut Below the Norm   77

9 Fire Walkers: Men on the Move   86

10 The Fraud of Endor   91

11 Look Into My Eyes As I Look Into Your Pocketbook   102

12 The Future Spoken—Compelling Evidence   121

13 Introduction to Demons and Angels   150

Source Notes   188

Foreword

The Ouija board, fortune-telling, ESP, mind reading, and so forth, are subjects that are batted about by people today with great regularity. Whether at the supermarket, a university classroom, street corner, or in a theological seminary—almost everyone has an active interest in paranormal experiences.

Those who are involved in the exercise of purported psychic phenomena seem to enjoy a position of power and notoriety in society. The media tends to give us the impression that those who exercise this "alleged ability" are unique and powerful individuals.

Many people harbor inaccurate concepts of the seemingly paranormal, which weaken their ability to understand and explain purported supernatural phenomena. It is amazing that there is not a single text written that separates the real from the fake, the genuine from the deceptive manipulations of the "fakers." Is there evidence for a supernatural world? It was for this reason I encouraged Danny Korem to write *The Fakers*. Few possess the skills and keen insight to expose the "fakers." I have personally seen Danny Korem demonstrate his ability as a magician, as well as having heard him speak on the material in this text. He is not only capable but credible. His selection of Dr. Paul Meier as coauthor gives a balance of medical and psychological expertise and insight and makes *The Fakers* an unusually convincing work. I am convinced that *The Fakers* will be a landmark text, making both Christians and non-Christians examine their perspectives of the supernatural and purported paranormal experiences. The evidence presented will compel the reader to seek out answers concerning the possibility of a God who directly intervenes in our daily lives.

Josh McDowell

Introduction

Nearly all of the phenomena dealt with in this book have been aired publicly through print, in lecture halls, and by the media. Unfortunately, the meat of most of the content that is valid is not common knowledge. There exist two extreme trends of thought in our society which are of equal danger: (1) the possibility of the supernatural does not exist; (2) many phenomena that actually originate in the physical are mistakenly believed to be of a supernatural nature. These mistaken philosophies exist in the realm of thought, from the scientific to the religious community, in spite of the facts. This text endeavors to give balance to the consideration of supernatural phenomena.

It was felt that the selection of a magician, a psychiatrist, and a leading researcher in the area of the supernatural, Mark Lundeen, would give this text the proper balance for approaching this subject. Many published, yet little-known, facts from both sides of the issue have been harnessed and put in a unique, new light. The conclusions we have drawn will cause both sides to adopt a more responsible perspective. We believe that when the text is taken as a whole, fresh new insights will be gained, and, most importantly, many fears of the supernatural will be laid to rest. Our effort is sincere, and the goal is to impart truth.

THE FAKERS

1
A Lesson in Deception

Visit any reputable bookstore, and you will find volumes of material on the occult. I recently did, and I asked the manager of a local store why so many books on this subject are sold, especially in light of the fact that most of the books available were obviously written to make money rather than to impart some truth. As we were talking, she pointed out an entire row of books by one author. She said that the material contained was "pure trash," but the author was very popular, and the books sell better than any others in the store.

With the massive amount of research that I have done over the past ten years, I have been able to locate only a handful of books that deal with the occult in a responsible and nonsensational manner. Many authors fabricate "true life" stories to build a reading audience; others, however, have been deceived into thinking that what they have witnessed or are reporting is actually of the occult when, in fact, they are reporting what I call *pseudo-occult* phenomena.

What is the difference between occult and pseudo-occult phenomena? Occult phenomena are phenomena of or relating to supernatural agencies, their effects, and knowledge of them. An example which many people consider a manifestation of occultic powers is demon possession. While the manifestation is visible, the force behind it is not. We can see the *effects* of a possession, but we cannot see the demon perpetrating the manifestation. Pseudo-occult phenomena are events which *appear* to be caused by secretive, supernatural powers and yet are brought about by physical or psychological means. An example of this is fire walking, which will be detailed in a later chapter.

One purpose of this book is to point out the difference between the occult and pseudo-occult. There is a great danger in treating both on an equal ground. One man who had reportedly performed the act of exorcism on several demon-possessed individuals tried his hand on a young teenager. The man strapped the young lady to a chair to prevent her from harming herself and proceeded with his ritual. It turned out that the girl was not demon possessed but was schizophrenic and needed the help of a trained psychiatrist. The girl, obviously terrified by the trauma, was left in worse shape than when she first went to see the man in question.

Misconceptions about the supernatural are legion, and it makes no difference whether one does or does not profess religious beliefs. Neither is one's level of mental competence or educational background a factor. In order for one to make qualified decisions as to whether an event is of the supernatural or not, it is helpful if one is schooled in the art of deception.

For the past eighteen years I have intensively studied the art of legerdemain, the art of sleight of hand. I make my living by entertaining people with magic *tricks*, as the lay public calls them, or *effects*, as they are labeled by fellow prestidigitators.

I have a saying that has held me in good stead: "You can fool all the people some of the time and some of the people all of the time, and that is sufficient!" A few well-meaning church members have criticized my doing magic by stating that the Bible explicitly speaks out against magicians. To clear the air, I went back to the original Hebrew and Greek texts. I discovered that the Hebrew word for magician is *chartom*, which means "one who draws magical lines or circles," which refers to a horoscopist.

In the New Testament, the Greek word for "sorcerer" (magician) is *pharmakos*, which means "one who gives potions." This is where we derive the word *pharmacy*. The rendering of the word *magician* in the Old and New Testaments always refers to one who is involved in occult or pseudo-occult practices.

Magic, as it is commonly used today, denotes a performer who entertains by presenting tricks of sleight of hand or through illusions. The word *magician*, as we know it today, did not even come into popular use until several hundred years ago. We used to be called jugglers because of the clever manipulative ability we could display with our hands. Only in a few rare cases do modern prestidigitators ever claim to have supernatural powers. Those who do are quickly exposed by other members of our trade. A recent example is Uri Geller, the purported psychic who claimed he could bend objects with his mind. He was exposed as a fraud by the knowledgeable and talented magician, James Randi, in his book *The Magic of Uri Geller*. It is possible, however, to convince almost anybody—under the right circumstances and through the use of trickery—that one may have supernatural powers. I made this point clear to several college buddies while I was attending Tulane University.

I argued that unless one is schooled in how the mind can be deceived, one is at a potential disadvantage when trying to objectively report so-called manifestations of occult powers. To illustrate my point, we went down to the pizza parlor on campus. I asked my friends to pick out someone who was eating by himself, and I would make that person believe that I was a visitor from the planet Pluto. They chose a fellow sitting in the corner of the restaurant. I bought a pizza and walked over to his table.

"Do you mind if I join you?" I asked.

"Sure. Have a seat," he replied.

Some small talk ensued for the next few minutes, and I then said, "I can't find my fork. Look! There it is." As I said this, I reached into the air and, by sleight of hand, produced the fork from thin air. His eyebrows raised so that they almost touched his receding hairline.

"Son of a gun. I forgot to get my ice water," I said. So I took my napkin and covered my hand with it. When I removed it, presto—the glass of ice water! When I placed it on the table, my newfound friend immediately grabbed it to make sure it was for real. I had also ordered a side order of olives. I took one of the olives in my right hand and placed it in the palm of my left hand. Closing my hand, I commented on the quality of the olives they served, and how much I liked olives. Slowly, I worked my hands back and forth, and when I opened them, all that was left was the pit. At this point this fellow was becoming profoundly disturbed.

"What are you, some sort of magician or something?" he asked.

"What are you talking about?" I replied.

"All the tricks you have been doing," he responded curiously.

"They aren't tricks," I stated.

"Well what are they?" he asked.

"Oh, you wouldn't believe me if I told you," I answered. As I said this, I pretended to notice some tomato sauce on my napkin. I folded it in half, and when I opened it, the spot was gone. It took a monumental effort to keep myself from rolling over with laughter as I witnessed the expressions on his face. Quickly, I changed the subject and temporarily halted the "miracles." Finally, after twenty minutes, with his curiosity eating him alive, he relented and asked, "Come on, what were you doing a few minutes ago?"

"If I told you, you wouldn't believe me," I stated as the cat-and-mouse game continued. "You'd probably laugh and think I was crazy," I added.

"Hey, man. Look at me. I'm serious. You have got to tell me what you are doing," he replied in earnest.

"Okay, you promise not to tell?" I asked, setting the hook.

"No, man. It stays with me," was his eager reply.

"I'm from Pluto, and I have my powers beamed down to me," I said with a straight face that would have rivaled any sculpted statue.

"You're kidding!" he blurted out.

"I told you that you wouldn't believe me." I snapped back.

"No, no, no. I believe you. It just sounds so incredible. Can you do something else?" he asked, wanting to believe.

I then proceeded to perform from my arsenal of impromptu tricks, seemingly causing objects to levitate, change form, and move invisibly from one place to another. He actually thought that I *was* from Pluto, and I thought that my friends, who had been quietly observing everything, were going to give it away.

To finish the story, the poor fellow avoided me whenever he saw me on campus. It took me three months to track him down long enough to tell him that I was not from Pluto. Fortunately, he is the only person I have ever tried to hoodwink into believing that I had supernatural powers. Someone else might not have lived through the experience.

Here is the whole point of the story. Given the proper circumstances, anyone can be made to believe that he has witnessed something which never took place as he *believed* it happened. When I present a trick, the lay public *knows* it is a trick and that I am a mere entertainer. This is readily apparent to my audience as I present on stage, my show, complete with one-liners, anecdotes, and bits of business. Now take me out of that setting and have me try to convince someone that I have powers, and most people will be convinced. In one of my acts, I perform what are called *mentalism* tricks. This is where I "apparently" read someone's mind and predict future events. Even though I tell the audience at the outset that everything they are about to witness is a trick, there are those who still believe some mystical power must come ito play. And only with repetitive reminders will these individuals leave my show knowing everything they have witnessed is a trick.

It is a false notion among laymen that a magician is able to fool his audience because the hand is quicker than the eye. For a magician to excel in his craft, he must first fool the mind and then fool the eye.

There are three levels of magic effects. The first is called the *puzzler*. This is a trick that fools only the eye, and the spectator can, with some thought, uncover the secret of the trick.

The second level is called the *fooler*. With a fooler the eye has been completely deceived and so has the mind, but the audience still knows that *something* must have happened. A typical example is when the magician produces a live dove from some silk handkerchiefs. You do not know *how* the magician got that dove, but you *know* it had to come from somewhere. Your mind and eye have been deceived, but you still know that *something* had to have happened.

The last level of trickery is called the *baffler*. This is what all top-flight magicians strive to present in their programs. The following is an example of a baffler I created as a closing number for one of my acts.

A spectator is chosen at random from the audience, and he is asked to collect several dollar bills from some people in the audience. From the collected bills, the spectator is then asked to choose one for the effect. The spectator is requested to copy down the serial number. (It must be pointed out that I never touch the dollar, at any time, nor does anyone else except the spectator, who is not a plant.) I ask the spectator to tear the dollar in half and place one of the halves in an envelope. (I never touch the envelope after I hand it to the spectator.) After the spectator places one half of the dollar in the envelope, he seals it, and then places it halfway in his pocket so that it is in plain view at all times. I hand my helper a lighter, and he visibly burns the other half of the bill. "The bill is now restored," I state, "and can be found in the envelope." The spectator rips open the envelope only to find the original half of the dollar that he sealed in the envelope moments ago.

"Are you sure the other half of the dollar is not in the envelope?" I ask.

"Yes. I am sure," is the reply.

"You won't believe it, but do you see that block of ice sitting on the table at the front of the stage?" I ask. Receiving an affirmative reply, I continue: "Frozen solid in that block of ice are two sheets of clear plastic which are secured together with rubber hands. Here is a hammer and an ice pick. Would you please chisel open the block of ice and remove the two sheets of plastic intact?" After a minute or so this is accomplished.

"You will notice that between the sheets of plastic is half of a dollar bill. It is not any dollar, but the match to the half you tore and burned a few minutes ago. Not only that, but when you separate the sheets of plastic, you will discover that the half of the dollar has been *laminated* between two sheets of plastic like a driver's license!" And exactly as I stated, the laminated half of the dollar which was frozen in the block of ice is the match to the half of a dollar the spectator sealed in the envelope which I never touched. And yes, the serial numbers match as well as the *tear*.

Many magicians, the first time they see this, are completely baffled. Laymen don't even have an inkling as to how I might have done the trick, and, more importantly, they don't even *sense* that I did anything at anytime that might in the least way be suspicious. *This* is the essence of the baffler.

I do not share this trick from my act to impress upon you how clever I am, but rather, that even a magician, one schooled in the art of deception, can be fooled. Were I to present this trick as a demonstration of supernatural powers and not as a trick, there are many people who would believe that they had witnessed a manifestation of some form of occult power. I know this for a fact.

Pat Boone followed me on a show where we were working together, and he said, "It is a good thing that Danny is on our side and told us that what he did was a trick, or we might have burned him at the stake!" His remark was followed by a round of nervous and relieved laughter.

The art of legerdemain is nothing more than a glorified con game. Its only purpose is to entertain. It is the pitting of one mind against another. Despite the vast amount of knowledge that I have, I can still be fooled by a magician who has developed a new principle or move. In the past three years, I have presented over thirty lectures to magicians in the United States and Canada. Many of the tricks completely fool the best in the business because I use their own knowledge against them. For example, a fellow might know that I have certain gimmicks that I like to use in accomplishing a particular effect. So what I will do is show him the trick without the gimmick, using another method, but fake like I *am* using the gimmick. At the end, he will realize that I did not use the gimmick suspected, and he will have been baffled. I have fallen prey to this ruse on many occasions when watching a fellow "finger flinger." This is what keeps our art interesting, even to those who know "the ropes." I do the same thing with a lay audience.

People always say that "it goes up your sleeve." If I hid as much stuff up my sleeve as people give me credit for, I would wear a bathrobe instead of an expensively tailored suit! I never hide anything up my sleeve. Today's fashions won't allow it. The sleeves would bulge. In a couple of tricks, the audience believes that something is concealed in my sleeve. So I pull up my sleeve *after* the real "work" has been done, thus leaving them without an explanation.

When learning a new trick, I am very sensitive as to how the spectator might think the trick is done. If the viewer *thinks* he knows how it is done, it is the same in his mind as if he *knows* how the trick is done. That is why I incorporate into my presentation that which will dispel the possible methods of how a trick might be done no matter how farfetched their explanation might be. If a sincere individual believes that he has witnessed a manifestation of some supernatural power—even when there was no supernatural power manifested—it is just as real in his mind, and he will be a difficult person to convince otherwise.

It is important in establishing the validity of my viewpoint that we look at the different methods by which one can be deceived. I will not reveal any intimate secrets of my craft, but I will explain the overall principles that are used to give you, the reader, the proper "feel." This will enable you to sense the working trickery even though you might not be able to detail the exact method. Although I do not endorse gambling, it is this kind of feel that would tell you how to stay in or get out of a crooked game. Knowing how you are being cheated is secondary to knowing that you are being cheated. By understanding the broad scope of how the mind can be fooled, you will understand why I look for and see certain things that other "qualified" scientists and researchers miss.

1. **Sleight of Hand.** This is the most obvious level of deception and requires the ability of the hands to act more *cleverly* than the eye or mind.

2. **Psychological Principles.** Here we deal with little-known idiosyncrasies in the way people think, and we then turn them to our advantage. For example, if you were to ask someone to think of a number between one and four, most people will say three. So, if you are clever, you can use this principle to present apparent demonstrations of mindreading.

3. **Using a Stooge.** This implies just what it says. Few magicians ever use a stooge because there is little need for one. However, when one is brought in, it catches everyone by surprise.

4. **Unseen and Unknown Devices.** These are gimmicks which exist, but the public is not aware of them. Many magicians, myself included, have developed pet items that utilize hidden devices, many of which are never revealed to fellow peers. One,

which is commonly known and seldom used today, is the gamblers *holdout*. It is a lazy-tongs type of mechanism that fits up the sleeve and delivers unseen several playing cards into one's hand. It can be operated by a slight movement of one's leg, or merely by inhaling or exhaling. A holdout can be purchased for about $600.

In an apparent demonstration of mind reading, Danny Korem, having asked a spectator to think of any card in a deck tossed into the audience, correctly "guesses" the card thought of.

5. **Mathematical Principles.** These are among the most commonly known by laymen and the least used by professional magicians. Many of these principles have been detailed in elementary magic books.

6. **Physics.** A while back, there was a trick whereby you could pour water from a pitcher into a drinking glass, and while it was pouring from the pitcher into the glass, the assistant would take out a pair of scissors and cut the stream of water. Part of the stream fell into the glass, and the upper part rose back into the pitcher. Those who did this trick did it as part of a routine with fluid. The

skulduggery was accomplished by adding to the water a chemical that was used in water-treatment plants to make the water more "slippery." There are many untapped principles of physics by which one can fool an audience.

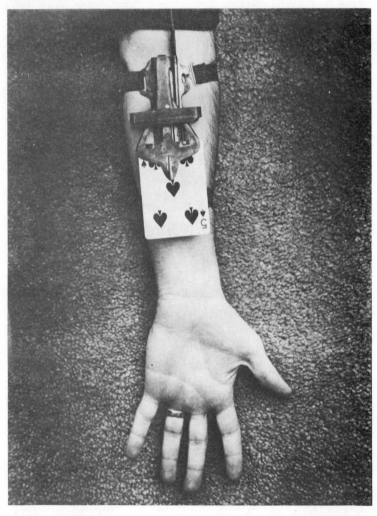

This is a card holdout, a device which delivers several playing cards into the hand unseen. The card is in a retracted state, the sleeve removed for demonstration purposes. *Photo courtesy of Bob White collection.*

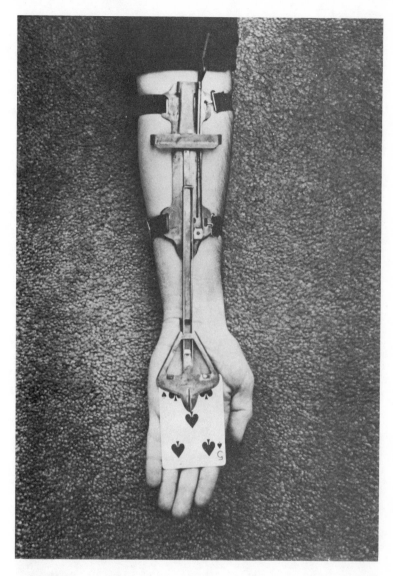

The holdout is activated by means of a connection from the unit to another part of the body, permitting the tripping of the device by a slight movement of one's leg or merely by inhaling or exhaling. *Photo courtesy of Bob White collection.*

7. **Physical Deception.**   The classic example is the escape from a length of rope. In 1979, I set the world's record by escaping from 1,680 feet of rope. That is more than 5 times the length of a football field. There were physical principles involved which insured my release after being bound. I am amused when people talk about

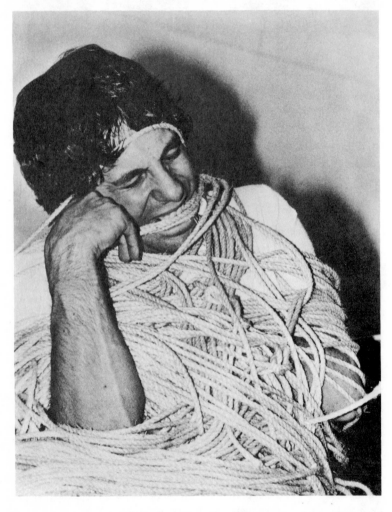

A classic example of physical deception is the escape from a length of rope. *Photo courtesy of St. Petersburg Times.*

Houdini shrinking his wrists to escape from handcuffs. Since the age of thirteen, I have been releasing myself from handcuffs. I can assure you of one thing: If Houdini did shrink his wrists, he would have either broken them or made medical history!

In 1979, Danny Korem set the world's record by escaping from 1680 feet of rope (more than 5 times the length of a football playing field). *Photo courtesy of St. Petersburg Times.*

8. **Mechanical Deception.** This is the second most obvious way to fool people. Gimmicklike boxes and apparatus fit into this category. Very few mechanical pieces look natural and therefore are seldom used by topflight professionals.

9. **Optical Illusion.** Rarely used. One example being sold today is a dome-shaped disc on which a penny apparently rests. When someone tries to pick up the penny, he discovers that the penny is actually sealed in the plastic dome.

Here the author has a page from a borrowed telephone directory, chosen by a spectator, who was asked to circle any number. The number is found to match a number Danny Korem had previously placed in a sealed envelope.

10. **Luck and Probability.** In this area, the performer is relying upon nothing but sheer luck, nerve, and some common sense. Last year, I went on a ski retreat with our church. If you have ever skied, you know how annoying a stopped ski lift can be. Such was our experience. After a couple of minutes, someone yelled out, "Danny, if you are a magician, why don't you get the lift going." "Okay," I yelled back. "Count to eighteen, and it will start again." I didn't have the foggiest idea when it would start up. Everyone started to count to eighteen, and, on the eighteenth beat, the lift started. Pure luck. When I looked back on my friend, he was kneeling! (I say this in jest, of course.) I have utilized this principle many times. When you miss, it is no big deal, because they didn't expect you to *hit*. And when you hit, you have performed, in their eyes, that which approaches the miraculous. Many of your so-called psychics, seers, fortune-tellers, and so forth, rely heavily on this principle.

11. **Combination of All the Principles.** By combining several principles, you make it very difficult for the layman to get a handle on the modus operandi of an effect.

How easy is it to be deceived? About a year ago, a young woman appeared on Johnny Carson's "Tonight Show." She claimed that through the use of bio-feedback and a special bio-rhythm machine she could present many uncanny demonstrations. To illustrate, she had Carson take and shuffle a deck of cards that the studio had purchased. She then removed a card from the deck and put it aside. Taking the shuffled deck, she scattered the cards haphazardly all over the table. "Touch any card," she told Carson. The card he touched turned out to be the perfect match of the card she set aside! She repeated this stunt over and over with the same results, regardless of how many times the participants decided to change their selection. What was so particularly amazing is that Carson is no slouch of a magician himself, and he was being completely taken. The last of her feats was the most amazing. She told Carson to touch the ace of spades. Unbelievably, from all the cards scattered across the table, he turned over the ace of spades. Truly amazing. How did she do it? I thought you would never ask!

As I stated once before, I cannot reveal secrets, because this is how I earn my living. I will never claim to be something that I am not, or that I possess powers I don't have. I later saw the same young woman at a magic convention in Wichita, Kansas, and she was demonstrating the identical tricks for a select group of magicians. I was getting a good laugh from the whole affair because this sweet and unassuming girl was baffling some of the best minds in the business. One of my friends asked me, "Danny, you do a lot of the psychological stuff, do you know what she is doing?"

"Yes, I have been doing that type of effect for several years," I replied.

"Well, what is she doing? You know me, I won't tip," he responded secretively.

I then proceeded to take my friend's deck of cards and exactly duplicate what we had seen. I then laid out the *works* of the effect. He said that what I had showed him was not what she presented. He didn't believe my explanation even after I demonstrated it for him! It wasn't until later that he realized that my description was accurate.

I sat with my friend in the back of the room while this innocent young lady confused the other magicians. I then proceeded to tell my friend the name of the card she was going to cause her subject to pick, and on whom she would force it. Then and only then would he believe me! The reason the magicians were so easily taken in was that she was using their own knowledge against them. Because she used several different methods, they were never able to reconstruct exactly *what* she was doing or *how* she was doing it. The point is this: If those trained and schooled in the art can be deceived by some very simple principles (a few of the fellows actually believed that she might have been using some kind of psychic power), then so can you.

When you see a purported seer or psychic performing on television or lecturing at a college campus, or you read of some extraordinary account, be skeptical.

In 1973, I had many newspaper reporters, television commentators, and radio announcers convinced that I might have some kind of psychic ability to predict the future. The events that I was going to try to "predict" were the bowl games on the coming New Year's Day. Two days before the scheduled games, I recorded my "impressions" of what I thought would be the final scores at the Rose, Sugar,

Cotton, and Orange Bowls. The piece of paper which listed my predictions was locked in the vault of a prominent downtown New Orleans bank. The vault used was one with a special time lock so that no one could enter the vault until after the games. The day after the games had taken place, the bank's president, surrounded by media people, opened the vault and the safe-deposit box which held the "prediction" slip secure. Lo and behold, the scores I had recorded were all accurate to the point except for one, and its numbers were reversed.

Remember, no one could discern how I was able to apparently predict the future events. I received more press coverage on the local newscast than Nixon did during the height of the Watergate affair. How was it done? I can't tell you. But I can tell you this: The whole thing was a trick. You might ask, "How can that be a trick?" I can't reveal the method because it is a principle of my craft. This much can be told: The illusion was created that there was a piece of paper in the vault and when the president opened the vault, the slip he removed was the same piece of paper. Now if you put two and two together, obviously somewhere and somehow there had to be a switch. But remember this, nobody but the president touched the piece of paper, and he was not a confederate. Neither did I use any other confederates or stooges. So again you ask, "How did you do it?" For $600 you might be able to purchase the secret from some exclusive magic shop.

I will not mention his name, but one of the leading professors of psychology in the United States was nearly convinced that I had some sort of a power when I attended Tulane University. I developed an imaginary theory called *SSP*, which stands for "Subtle Sensory Perception." It was by my utilization of this fraudulent theory that I claimed to be able to accomplish many feats of purported precognition (ability to predict the future), telepathy, and so forth. I received reams of letters from all sorts of characters. One man, a gambler, offered me $10,000 if I would correctly give him the score of the 1973 Super Bowl. Others asked me to help locate lost relatives, jewelry, and drowning victims. How desperate people are to seek direction.

Because of the uproar produced by my stunts, I decided to expose what I was doing by letting the media know that it was being accomplished through trickery. Today, when I present a similar demonstration, I explain that what I am doing *is* a trick and that I am merely presenting it for the entertainment of my audience. Following such a show, I conclude with a talk debunking much of what the lay public thinks is occult phenomena. In the past few years, I have exposed many purported psychics and seers as I realize the danger they pose.

At the beginning of this chapter, I stated that one purpose of this book is to differentiate between occult and pseudo-occult phenomena. The reader, because of my perspective may assume that I have ruled out the possibility of the intervening of supernatural agents in the flow of day-to-day existence. I *do* believe such intervention can and does take place. I do *not* believe that man *in and of his own power and volition* can manifest supernatural powers, i.e. telepathy, psychokinesis (the ability to mentally move objects), precognition, and so forth. I *do* believe that all supernatural powers are derived from only two sources, which will be detailed later in the text. The goal of this treatise is not only to debunk much of what is considered supernatural phenomena, but *also* to come full circle and identify those supernatural powers that do exist and their origins.

In order to present my case, I have rigidly examined all case studies, utilizing a legalistic, historical perspective. I examined the physical evidence, written testimony, and the oral testimony of those who may have been involved in each case. Much testimony has been discarded because, in my opinion, either the person providing the testimony had an axe to grind, or might have intentionally—or unintentionally—tried to distort the facts. Outside of my own personal data, I will rely heavily on three other sources.

The first man is Milbourne Christopher, one of the leading magicians in the world. He is past president of the Occult Investigative Committee for the Society of American Magicians (SAM). The SAM is a leading organization for magicians that has boasted such members as Houdini, Howard Thurston, Blackstone, and others. It is interesting to note that although Mr. Christopher has devoted many years of research to phenomena of a potentially occultic nature, he has never witnessed that which could be considered "legitimate."

D. H. Rawcliffe, one of the foremost authorities on the occult and pseudo-occult, will be relied upon as another primary source of information. Many of my independent findings have corresponded with Mr. Rawcliffe's.

Dr. Kurt Koch will be the third individual whose writings I will use for illustrative purposes. Despite over twenty thousand case studies which Dr. Koch has personally researched and reported, many of his findings are questionable, even though his intentions are sincere. As a pastor, he is heavily involved in counseling those who had contact or influence with purported occult phenomena.

It is important for the reader to understand that I do not align myself with any of the individuals quoted in this book. Instead, I use their studies and research to make a statement of my belief in this highly volatile area.

A word of caution must be exercised: Do not prejudge the material in this book in light of your own experiences or the experiences of those about whom you may have read. One must be trained in order to be able to discern between that which is of the supernatural and that which is not. Few people like to admit that they have been hoodwinked or deceived. If Sir Arthur Conan Doyle, a former astronaut, leading researchers at Stanford Research Institute in California, and other prominent and respected persons have been fooled into thinking that a particular event was brought about legitimately by one masquerading as a psychic, so can you and other credible people.

After innumerable lectures on this subject, I am convinced that the fear of supernatural phenomena, which most people have, will be laid to rest. Most phenomena are of the physical and not of the supernatural. In the supernatural realm, powers are derived from either the Creator or Satan. If a rarely produced manifestation is of the Lord who created us, there is no need for fear. And if the phenomenon is satanically produced, the Christian has ultimate power over it.

We will begin with the simplest of phenomena, and then move to those which are more complex. We ask the reader to utilize the information in this text in a responsible manner.

Danny Korem

PSYCHIATRIC COMMENT

It took thirteen years of higher education for me to become a psychiatrist. The primary subject I mastered during that extensive training period was the subject of human self-deception. I studied extensively the forty most common human *defense mechanisms* by which all 4 billion humans on planet Earth deceive themselves daily from the truth. My patients are "set free" from many of their emotional conflicts by discovering the truth about their behavior, thinking, and emotions, and then by giving up various defense mechanisms. Most family doctors I know tell me that from 60 to 80 percent of their patients primarily have emotional needs, even though they present physical complaints. I have successfully treated hundreds of my own patients who have real illnesses, such as arthritis and high blood pressure. Through the use of suggestion, I have also "cured" many patients of imagined illnesses, such as blindness, paralysis, hypoglycemia, epilepsy, and multiple sclerosis.

In addition, I have treated hundreds of patients who came to me reporting that they were demon possessed. Patients have told me of hearing audible voices from demons, from God, from angels, and so forth. They have had "visions" from God and "answers to the problems of the universe." However, out of these hundreds of cases, none of them ended up being legitimate cases of demon possession. Any halfway-knowledgeable psychiatrist, Christian or non-Christian, knows that delusions and hallucinations are associated with an abnormal level in the brain's biochemistry. We merely give the patient a major tranquilizer (antipsychotic agent), restoring the dopamine level to normal, and all those "demon voices," visions, and so forth go away within a few weeks.

Allow me to give you a few actual case studies to illustrate what I mean. (Only the names have been changed.)

Case 1. Martha M. was a deacon's wife in a healthy, Bible-believing, local church. She was well liked, attractive, and the godly mother of three children. She got along well with her husband, who was also very respected in their community.

One night Martha started hearing voices coming from nowhere, which told her that her husband was planning to kill her. She was, of course, shocked by this, but the voices seemed so real she believed them and didn't tell her husband about it. After she and her husband went to bed, the voices told her that she was God in the flesh and that her husband was plotting to "crucify" her that night. She slipped out of her bed to get a butcher knife to kill her husband in self-defense. However, he woke up before she could stab him, and overpowered her. He called their pastor, who came immediately to help out. The pastor, an experienced counselor himself, recognized the case as a simple psychotic break rather than demon possession (which her husband suspected).

Together, they brought Martha to the hospital emergency room where I saw them and admitted Martha. After two days on large doses of a major tranquilizer, Martha was totally back to normal, with no delusions or hallucinations. She was very embarrassed and scared about the fact that she had nearly killed her husband because of temporary insanity.

Over the next few weeks, Martha and I dealt with her severe passivity and feelings of inferiority, stemming from improper nurturing by her parents in early childhood. She meditated on passages of Scripture that built up her self-worth, such as Psalm 139. She was cured without exorcism. That doesn't mean that demons may not have been getting her so down on herself that she had to "flip out" and think she was God to bear the pain of her insignificance, but she wasn't demon possessed. A Christian cannot be demon possessed anyway, since 1 Corinthians 10:13 tells us we are never tempted more than we can bear. God's Word also reassures Christians that "greater is he [the Holy Spirit] that is in you, than he [Satan] that is in the world" (1 John 4:4).

Case 2. Karen K. was a UCLA college senior who suddenly went totally blind, forcing her to drop out of school. She was seen by the best neurologists in America, who could find no organic basis for her blindness. Her primary neurologist referred her to me for psychiatric evaluation. She was not faking her blindness but had actually deceived herself into believing she was blind. If obstacles were placed in her path, she would fall over them and become bruised from the fall.

Illnesses of this nature are very common. They can be seen in many "faith healing" services. They are called *hysterical conversion reactions*. This does not disclaim the fact that God can and does supernaturally heal real illnesses, because He does.

I merely used the power of suggestion on Karen by telling her to go take a nap. I told her that when she woke up from the nap, she would be able to see again. Because she believed me, it worked. She took a nap right away, and when she woke up, her vision was restored for the first time in several months.

Case 3. Byron D. was admitted to my care because of depression, but he also had had epilepsy for years. His family doctor had him on phenobarbital and Dilantin for his seizure disorder. Since about 20 percent of epileptics don't really have epilepsy, but rather have hysterical seizures, I decided to check him out with an EEG (brain-wave test). His EEG was normal, so I weaned him off his epilepsy drugs. Whenever he had a hysterical seizure, we ignored him, rather than give him the great attention his mother always did during these times. Within three weeks, he was over his "epilepsy" and he never has had a seizure since then.

Case 4. Donald C. was about to be medically discharged from the army because it was thought he had developed multiple sclerosis. I was asked to examine him (psychiatrically) in a Veterans Hospital. He really thought he was paralyzed from MS, but after a negative colloidal gold spinal-fluid study and extensive psychological and neurological testing, we concluded that he was suffering from a hysterical conversion reaction. With a few weeks of therapy, he was cured of his imaginary multiple sclerosis and was back on his feet. However, he then needed long-term psychotherapy to assist him in living up to his responsibilities. He was so lazy that his mind tricked him into "developing" MS so he could avoid responsibility without feeling guilty about it.

From the above case studies, one can begin to comprehend how easily deceived and naive we humans really are. What happened to those patients in my actual case studies happens to nearly all of us humans, although usually to a lesser extent. When we get angry and don't want to be aware of it, we merely develop headaches instead to keep our minds away from our true hurt. If we don't like someone, we merely trick ourselves into believing that person does not like us. If we deny our own blind spots, we reject and criticize others who have similar faults, even though theirs may be much less severe than our own. (See Matthew 7:1-5 for an excellent description of this type of human deception.) If we feel extremely inferior on an unconscious level, we merely delude ourselves into thinking we are great, perhaps even God in the flesh.

Paul Meier, M.D.

2
A Twitch Is the Snitch

In his book *He is There and He Is Not Silent* Francis A. Schaeffer, one of the world's brilliant thinkers, ponders the question of why men look for mystical answers to very real questions. In the present flow of humanistic thinking, man has eliminated the possibility of a Divine Creator and leans toward the chance beginning and evolution of man. This means that because man is a product of chance, so too is his thinking. Man's inherent finiteness eliminates the possibility of his making authoritative statements concerning that which is infinite. Yet there is a great yearning in modern man for that which supercedes his own knowledge and experience, and hence a yearning for that which is supernatural, or "upstairs" experiences, as Dr. Schaeffer refers to them. The following quote is an incisive view of man's longing for the mystical.

> So man makes his leap "upstairs" into all sorts of mysticisms in the area of knowledge—and they *are* mysticisms, because they are totally separated from all rationality. This is a mysticism like no previous mysticism. Previous mysticisms always assumed something was there. But modern man's mysticisms are semantic mysticisms that deal only with words; they have nothing to do with anything being there, but are simply concerned with something in one's own head, or in language in one form or another. The modern taking of drugs began as one way to try to find meaning within one's head.[1]

There are many other reasons for the rise in interest in occult and pseudo-occult phenomena. Os Guiness, in his book *Encircling Eyes* creatively deals with this by stating that he always attempts to avoid an overskeptical rationalism, on one hand, or any premature escape into a magical explanation, on the other. He later continues:

A good illustration of the necessary balance can be seen in the relation of herbalism to modern medicine. Moldy cheese was once applied as a cure for festering sores. Whether man believed this was supernatural magic or whether it was merely a superstition, we now know that they were simply stumbling on a primitive application of penicillin. Foxgloves were once used for heart ailments, but modern medicine has isolated digitalis from the foxglove and uses it as a stimulant in modern heart drugs. Indians once used the rauwolfia root to cast out strange spirits, and pharmacology now uses some of the substance from this root in the manufacture of tranquilizers. This plainly underlines the necessity of examining each phenomenon in the light of all the various possible implications, thus avoiding extreme interpretations on either side, directed by one's prior premises and not be the facts in question.[2]

Mr. Guiness states what he believes are eight of the major contributing reasons for so much serious consideration to that which is of a mystical and supernatural nature.

1. THE DEATH OF RATIONALISM—Rationalistic thought played down the possibility of mystical elements.... Twentieth-century rationalism has stumbled, its wings severely clipped by psychoanalysis and modern philosophy. The door to the nonrational, the irrational and superrational is wide open.
2. INCREASING RECOGNITION OF MYSTERY IN MODERN PHYSICS
3. PRESENT STATE OF PSYCHIC AND PARAPSY-CHOLOGICAL RESEARCH
4. SKEPTICISM TOWARDS THE SUPERNATURAL IN LIBERAL THEOLOGY
5. THE INFLUENCE OF EASTERN RELIGIONS

6.   THE CHAOS AND COMPLEXITY OF MODERN
     CULTURE
7.   FOR THE CHRISTIAN THE SUPERNATURAL REALLY
     DOES EXIST—Within the Christian framework there is not
     so much a natural and supernatural world, as if the natural
     were the real and the supernatural the less real; rather there
     is a seen and unseen world, and both have *equal reality.*
8.   THE FAILURE OF ATHEISM TO PRODUCE CON-
     CRETE ANSWERS[3]

I highly recommend Mr. Guiness's excellent treatise for a detailed
analysis of these eight convincing arguments.

What I find appalling is the apparent abandonment of faith in order
to believe in many types of pseudo-occult phenomena. In this
section, we will deal with pseudo-occult phenomena that are of a
physical nature. You will find some of the phenomena amusing *after*
you know how they are brought about. The intense belief of those
who are uninformed is staggering.

Mentalism, as stated earlier, is that branch of legerdemain where
one is apparently able to read someone's mind, prognosticate future
events, and cause one spectator to seemingly read another
spectator's mind. One area of mentalism involves that which is called
muscle reading. This is the ability of locating hidden objects with
"apparently" nothing but the mind. Many performers of the past and
present have featured this remarkable trick.

J. Randall Brown, in the late 1800s, could locate a needle hidden
anywhere within walking distance in a city. Another was Franz J.
Polgar. Milbourne Christopher, in his book *ESP, Seers and
Psychics*, relates these examples:

> For many years this effective finale was the climax of Franz J. Polgar's
> routine. Despite the trepidations of his agent, who constantly feared
> he might lose his commission, the Hungarian-born showman never
> missed. During Polgar's cross country tours he found his elusive
> checks in some unlikely places. Once he took a rolled-up check from
> the gun of a Texas police chief; another time he found one which had

been sealed in a tennis ball. He didn't hesitate to break open the hollowed out heel of a woman's slipper, which had been glued back in place containing the tightly folded paper, but he was reluctant to reach for another check which had been hidden in a girl's brassiere.

Look magazine, in December 1950, pictured the short, grayhaired thought reader staring up at the Empire State Building in New York. A small silver banknote clip had been stashed away somewhere in the 102-story structure. Another picture disclosed that Polgar had found the object of his search in a subbasement locksmith shop. It had been tucked in the lower metal drawer of a metal file case![4]

For many years those who could present this trick were thought to possess psychic powers. Although I cannot give away all of the "works," I will give you enough of a headstart so that you will know that this is a trick and should you witness a demonstration, you will know it is not of the supernatural.

In the late 1800s, a Russian psychologist, J. Tarchanow, and an American psychologist, J. Jastrow, were both doing independent tests on what is called *ideomotor action*. The term, while not widely used today, referred to uncontrollable muscular actions which are a direct response to conscious or unconscious thoughts. To prove their theory, each man developed his own type of testing apparatus. What follows is a report of the device that Jastrow invented and the results he achieved as they were recorded in the book *Occult and Supernatural Phenomena* by D. H. Rawcliffe.

Jastrow's apparatus was simple: a square wooden frame contained a plate of glass upon which were placed three polished steel balls. These balls support another framed plate of glass. Attached to the upper frame was a rigid rod which terminated in a recording apparatus. A complete record of every movement of the upper glass frame could thus be traced upon sheets of glazed paper by this means.

To use this automatograph, or tremograph, the subject places the tips of his fingers upon the glass plate which is supported by the three ballbearings. It is virtually impossible to hold the plate still for more than a few seconds, particularly if a screen renders the subject's hand invisible to its owner. Under these conditions the subject is instructed to think as little as possible of his hand, and at the same time to make a reasonable effort to prevent it from moving. As long as the subject's attention is not fixed upon anything in particular, the resulting involuntary shaky movements of his hand produce a random meaningless pattern on the recording apparatus. But if the subject's attention is fixed on some object in the room, the pattern produced is that of an irregular line whose general direction lies towards the focus of attention. Again, if the subject is directed to count silently the ticks of a metronome, or even merely to watch its movements, the record shows that his hand moves to and fro—not accurately but in a general way—in time with the instrument. Tarchanow's experiments showed that if his subjects concentrated for any length of time upon an object, the resultant pattern showed "sometimes the figure of a square, sometimes the figure of a triangle or a circle, according to the dominant form of the object." With geometric figures this tendency was even more marked.

In one of Jastrow's experiments the subject was asked to concentrate his attention for thirty-five seconds upon some patches of color on the wall opposite. Without warning, the subject was then directed to count the strokes of a metronome for the same length of time. The sudden change completely altered the style of the ideomotor movements as revealed by the automatograph. Jastrow and Tarchanow both found that unconscious ideomotor actions manifested themselves in slight movements of the whole body, generally in the form of irregular swaying. By fixing the apparatus to the subject's head the movements could be recorded. It was found that in regard to these slight swaying movements there was a general movement toward the object of attention.[5]

I have used the principle of ideomotor action since I was in high school. I purchased a book at a magic shop and learned how to find objects hidden at random in a room by friends. It made for a great party stunt. By now I am sure you are on to how this trick might be done. After the object is hidden and the performer returns to the room, he takes the most excited female who knows the location of the object, and holds her hand. As he circles the room he asks her to think hot or cold. When he moves in the direction where the object is hidden, there is little resistance in her hand. When he moves away from the object there is a slight resistance in her hand as he pulls her along. Slight changes in breathing, a slight hesitation in the walk, a slight flushing of the skin, all contribute to the "reading" of the helper's responses. One of the greatest tip-offs is the audience. As one gets closer to the object, the audience quiets down because they don't want to give away the location of the object. When one moves further away, they start talking. They figure that the performer will never find it, so why pay close attention! There are many other factors involved, and it takes many years of practice to become an expert at muscle reading. Even if a person knows how the trick is done, it is still amazing to see it performed.

I have taken the same principle and carried it one step further. There are times when I receive a long distance phone call and a booker wants to know, "Are you as good as your promo?" I ask the prospect to take out some playing cards and spread them across the table and to turn over one card and think of it, then turn it face down in its original position. I then ask him to call out the names of all the cards spread in front of him. Without asking a single question, I tell him the name of the card he is merely thinking of! You might ask how can this principle be applied to a trick done over the telephone. You just have to take my word that it can be done. This particular stunt has baffled many magicians. Here I have taken a well-known principle, cloaked in a different presentation, and baffled those who knew the secret but were not aware of it. Many fraudulent psychics take principles of legerdemain, cloak them in a presentation of apparent psychic phenomena, and lo and behold, a new psychic is born. This section on muscle reading is the simplest to comprehend readily. Keep the idea of ideomotor action locked in your mind as we proceed to the pendulum.

Danny Korem

PSYCHIATRIC COMMENT

What Danny Korem is saying about body language is absolutely accurate. As a psychiatrist, one of my primary responsibilities is to uncover unconscious conflicts, which are blind spots that the patient is not even aware of. I uncover these simply by having gut-level conversations with my patients about various possible areas of conflict. When we happen to hit upon conflicts that are causing them anxiety, they will have an autonomic nervous-system response without even noticing it themselves. The pupils of their eyes dilate, their necks blotch in pink blotches, their hand muscles tense up, and their hands may sweat somewhat. They frequently will change their posture in a symbolic manner in an effort to protect themselves from finding out the truth, since the truth usually hurts. They do this by crossing their arms, looking away from me (frequently toward the floor), and crossing one leg over another, away from wherever I am sitting. Their unconscious minds, in an effort to deceive themselves from the truth, give the truth away through this automatic, unconscious, autonomic nervous-system response.

When the patient becomes painfully aware of the truth, verbalizes the blind spot (such as repressed anger toward a parent), and takes a positive plan of action to deal with it, his anxiety goes away. This is how well-trained psychiatrists relieve their patients of years of anxiety and depression.

Paul Meier, M.D.

3
The Pendulum—Belief Suspended

For some reason an object that is swinging by a wire, cord, or string always creates attention. Edgar Allan Poe developed a terrifying story around a pendulum in his famous tale "The Pit and the Pendulum." At a recent magic convention, a friend of mine put on a swami outfit and stood in the lobby of a prestigious Houston hotel and "commanded" a huge steel ball suspended by a ninety-foot cable—which had been hung for decorative purposes—to begin to move "at his every command." To the amazement of all, the ball did begin to swing. Or did it? He then ordered the ball to continue to swing until he left the hotel three days later. Many people checked to see if the ball was still swinging every morning on the way to breakfast, and sure enough it was. What they didn't know is that it was moving all the time. But nobody stands in the lobby of a hotel to check to see if one of the ornamental fixtures is moving. My friend had a lot of people going. And he also had a lot of laughs.

Those who suspend an object by a string and try and divine answers of the future are called "radiathesiasts." The term *radiathesiast* was coined because it was believed that the object over which a pendulum was suspended gave off waves or some form of radiation which caused muscular movements in the hand of the person holding it, thus causing the movement of the pendulum. One of the earliest records of a radiathesiast was recorded by the Roman historian Ammianus Marcellinus.

The direction of movement of a pendulum, allowed to swing freely as shown here, is thought by some to indicate answers to questions. The movement of the pendulum, however, is simply a manifestation of ideomotor action—uncontrollable muscular actions that are direct responses to conscious or unconscious thoughts.

> He records that in the time of the Emperor Valens a number of men were arrested and condemned to death for endeavoring to divine the name of the Emperor's successor. The method they used was to set the letters of the alphabet out in a circle, as in a modern Ouija board, and to suspend a ring over the center of the circle. The ring, by the direction of its swing indicated in turn various letters of the alphabet.[6]

It is amazing to what absurd lengths man will go to try to see into the future. In addition to being able to divine the future, the radiathesiast is supposed to: (1) be able to tell whether a person is lying or not; (2) be able to locate hidden objects, such as buried treasure or water beneath the surface of the ground; (3) be able to divine simple yes or no answers; (4) divine, by holding the object suspended over the abdomen of a pregnant woman, whether the unborn child will be a boy or a girl.

My first contact with the pendulum was in an ESP game my parents bought for me that had been put out by Kreskin, a prominent mentalist (magician who does mentalism tricks). An egg-shaped object was attached to a six-inch length of chain. One held the end of the chain between the forefinger and thumb while his elbow rested on the table, allowing the egg-shaped object to be suspended above the tabletop. Then by asking the pendulum a question, one would learn the answer. If the pendulum swung in a circle, the answer was yes. If it swung in a straight line, the answer was no.

I made practical use of this bit of nonsense. My younger sister was notorious for stealing candy from my mother's pantry. When questioned about taking it, she always denied the dastardly deed. Being the oldest of the clan, I was expected to keep my two brothers and two sisters in line. Utilizing the principle of ideomotor action, I put the pendulum to work. If you allow the object attached to the string to swing freely while you are not thinking about anything, the pendulum will swing in a circle. When one is asked a yes-or-no question, if the truth is spoken, the pendulum will continue to swing in a circular pattern. If one lies, however, an uncontrollable and imperceptible twitch will be given off by your hand, thus disrupting the orbit of the object and causing it to swing in a straight line. Unfortunately for my little sister, she was caught, and "justice" prevailed.

Many people believe, contrary to fact, that the pendulum contains or allows the release of some occult power. What follows are three quotes from Dr. Koch's works on cases where he has studied manifestations that he believes are caused by the pendulum:

> An expectant mother allowed a pendulum practitioner to use a pendulum over her unborn child to determine whether it was a boy or girl. Both the woman's children were treated in this way and today they are both oppressed and burdened as a result of it.[7]

A postal employee has the ability to find water when using a divining rod or a pendulum, and he can always correctly identify the position of telephone cables with the pendulum. He has commented, however, on signs of tiredness appearing after his dowsing.[8]

A young man, being out of work, has a pendulum practitioner find jobs for him by using the pendulum over the "Vacant Jobs" column of a newspaper. In this way he had the offer of five jobs in one day. But although he got a job immediately, after a few days he had to give it up again because he became emotionally disturbed. He then spent some months in a mental hospital. When his health improved he turned to some monks for advice. Again he was told to seek the help of a pendulum practitioner. Finally, he sought the counsel of a magic charmer. The result was that a few days later he had attacks of temporary insanity and was again taken to the mental hospital.[9]

These cases all sound very sensational and might cause fear for the wrong reason. I do not advise the use or the pursuit of any of the pseudo-occult phenomena that will be discussed in this book—not because they possess any hidden power but because they further superstitious practices and encourage individuals to seek direction outside of the God who created them. Many Christians believe that this kind phenomenon is satanic, that is, the pendulum is moved by demons or Satan. This is not true. There is no need for Satan or his cohorts to move the pendulum because the operator, due to ideomotor action, will move the pendulum the way he consciously or unconsciously wants it to move. Satan's purpose, as born out by the scriptural record, is to have man turn from God and seek his *own* direction rather than that of the Lord. The pendulum aids in this goal. It furthers Satan's purpose if a man will believe that some inanimate object has some mystical power. This is a form of idol worship disdained in the Bible.

In the cases mentioned, one might be led to believe that there are certain cause-and-effect relationships that are a direct result of using a pendulum. I have already explained how the pendulum can be used as a primitive (and not inerrable) lie detector. Can one locate objects? The answer is no. It has never been proven scientifically on a repeated basis. The answering of yes-or-no questions, discerned by the movement of the pendulum, is simply a manifestation of ideomotor action. Following several lectures, I have had women tell me that their doctor could guess with uncanny accuracy whether their child would be a boy or a girl. I call to their attention that if you had a hundred doctors and each made a hundred random guesses concerning the sex of unborn children, some, by the laws of probability, would have a higher "hit" ratio than others. My wife is a registered nurse and works in a labor and delivery unit, and she assures me that—except by medical means—there is no way to discern the sex of an unborn child.

Milbourne Christopher relates an amusing story of a man who claimed that he could diagnose illnesses using the pendulum.

> Another French medical man, E. Pascal, investigated a Bordeaux diviner who claimed his instrument worked as well over a few hairs as over a patient's body. Pascal brought him several black strands and watched his procedure. Suspending the pendulum with one hand, the rhabdomancer [another name for diviner] moved a pencil in the other hand over an anatomy chart. When the weight traveled in a circle, he said this indicated the organ was sound. A straight back-and-forth swing denoted illnesses. His final diagnosis was that the hairs belonged to a young man who was in a feverish condition. His pharynx was weak; his blood was infected by coli bacilli; and he had carcinoma of the pancreas. The hairs, however, were not from a human; they had been plucked from a healthy bulldog.[10]

You can see from the above story that if one truly did put his faith in one of these diviners, the results could be disastrous. Concerning Dr. Koch's cases, let us consider each one separately.

The story of the mother with the two oppressed children has no clear-cut cause-and-effect relationship. Dr. Koch makes the assumption that because of the passing of the pendulum over the unborn children, they became oppressed and burdened. The pendulum in and of itself possesses no power. I suspect that these children would have grown up the same regardless of the passing of the pendulum—providing the mind-set of the mother was the same. It was probably the deprived nature of the mother that sent her to a pendulum practitioner and provided the negative influence on her children. And then again it could have been a totally unrelated set of circumstances that led to the children's mind-set. I call this kind of a story a *building* story. You put it amongst several other stories that appear to be credible, and it makes a less credible story appear more valid.

The story of the postal worker also lacks credibility from a reporting point of view. As stated in the first chapter, I use the legalistic, historical method for reporting past events. One must review the physical facts, check written testimony, and screen oral testimony. None of these factors are treated serious by Dr. Koch. It is not a proven fact that the postal worker could indeed find water or telephone cables with any better accuracy than anyone else who made guesses by pure chance. (In the next section, Mr. Christopher's amusing story lays to rest the purported ability to find water or telephone cables or any other object.) Dr. Koch adds, as a kind of aside, that the gentlemen in question noticed "signs of tiredness appearing after his dowsing," leading one to believe that the pendulum sapped some of his physical energy. Of course the man was tired. You would be, too, if you had to find water and cables while stooped over the ground, waiting for the swing of some object to tell you if you had hit or not—and especially if you had a fear of being proven a fool by making a mistake!

No doubt, by pure chance, one might be able to locate objects, discern ailments, predict the sex of an unborn child, and any other task your heart might fancy to pursue. But the question is this: Does the pendulum have any supernatural power? The obvious answer is no. I have noticed a trait in individuals who pursue these kinds of pseudo-occult fantasies. When they do hit, they feel very important, because they have accomplished something, in their minds, which the rest of the populace is unable to accomplish. And due to the "secretive" nature of how their "instruments" operate, these individuals take on a mystical quality with those who want to believe that this sort of phenomenon is a supernatural occurrence. From the

Christian point of view, this is very harmful, because these individuals believe they have the "power" and can seek their own direction instead of seeking the power and knowledge of an almighty God. Thus Satan's purpose has been accomplished without the manifestation of any supernatural powers.

Danny Korem

PSYCHIATRIC COMMENT

Insecure persons crave anything that will make them feel significant. Having some special power would be fantastic, especially for certain personality types, such as the histrionic (hysterical) or paranoid, who tend to be the most naive.

The kind of reasoning used in Dr. Koch's examples is incredible! If this kind of reasoning were accurate, I could say that since a dog was urinating on a tree while I was reading a newspaper column on football, my reading of the football article must have caused the dog to urinate. This type of insane reasoning is called *ideas of reference* in psychiatric terminology. Most humans probably have mild ideas of reference, such as cheering during a football game to try to effect the outcome. It gives us a false feeling of power. Ideas of reference, when more severe, are a sign of schizophrenic or preschizophrenic thought.

Paul Meier, M.D.

4
The Dowsers Take a Dunking

Part of the folklore of the state of Texas, where I live, relates to those legendary people who have the "gift" of being able to find water by what is called dowsing.

The term, to "dowse," most likely originated in the sea-bound peninsula of Cornwall where the use of the forked rod was introduced by German miners during the days of Queen Elizabeth in order to prospect for tin. The term has a variety of meaning in Cornwall, but its connection with ore and water divination probably derived from the widespread colloquialism to "dowse a sail," meaning to lower sail, the word borrowed to describe the dipping action of the divining rod.[11]

On a local talk show a few months back, the hosts of the show, with an aura of amazement, aired a clip about a Maryland man who could seemingly discover—by dowsing—the underground whereabouts of water, in areas where trained well drillers had failed. The commentator, referring to the man's "gift"—implying that he had a power that most do not possess—stated that nobody knows how or why his ability works. The clip proceeded to show the man taking a forked branch from a tree, holding it in his hands, and walking across a grassy field. Then, mysteriously, the tip of the forked rod dipped down, signaling that water was beneath that spot. The gentleman then gave the reporter the rod and asked her to try her hand at it. Tense seconds passed and, believe it or not, nothing happened. The reporter shook her head, filled with the wonderment of the "gift" this man seemingly possessed. She stated that in the dowser's hands it was impossible to keep the rod from dipping down toward the ground. To illustrate, the gentleman stood over the spot where the rod began to dip, and, as it did, the reporter tried to stop the downward movement by holding the tip of the rod and pulling it up. The rod, as if it were alive, snapped in half rather than yield to the upward force of the reporter's hand.

To conclude the story, the dowser demonstrated his water-finding ability with two L-shaped welding rods as well as a pair of pliers. The reporter, with an air of authority, stated that dowsing had been used in Vietnam to find land mines although she did not state how successful it had been. It should be noted that during the demonstration there was never any mention of whether water was actually discovered at the spots where the rod or pliers dipped or if water was or was not plentiful in the area, or if the man did or did not have prior knowledge of underground wells.

Before unveiling the modus operandi behind this primitive method of finding water, let me share this account from Dr. Koch's writings:

> A Christian wanted to discover if there was a spring in his large garden. A dowser had reactions in two places but no water was found on digging there. The dowser was surprised and said, "This has never happened to me before." The Christian man in reply said that he had prayed about the matter beforehand, since he had not been sure whether he as a Christian should have called a dowser in to help or not. "Well, that's why," replied the dowser. "Of course it wouldn't work."[12]

Let us first deal with what causes the rod to dip and apparently locate an underground source of water. Again, we may look to ideomotor action as the culprit. During the film clip mentioned, I paid close attention to see if my suspicions would be confirmed, and they were. If you will examine the photograph, you will notice that my thumbs are extended from the fists which are tightly clenched around the rod. By applying pressure with the thumbs against the rod, it can be caused to dip. For most diviners this is an unconscious action. The rod can also be caused to dip by a slight turning of the

Dowsing refers to the search for underground water by means of a dowsing rod, often a forked branch, the tip of which dips down to signal that water is beneath the spot. This picture of Danny Korem shows the position in which one televised dowser held the branch. Notice the position of the thumbs, extended from the fists which are tightly clenched around the rod.

wrists. The reason the rod broke when the reporter tried to halt the downward movement of the rod was due to the leverage the diviner had over the reporter. He was using two hands and two prongs of the rod to cause the rod to dip, while the reporter could only hold onto the tip of the rod. Common sense will tell you that the diviner was exerting twice as much force as the reporter, so the weakest part of the rod had to give, and this was the tip.

Here you can see that only slight pressure of the thumbs against the rod is needed to cause the branch to dip down where water is thought to be beneath the surface. For most diviners this is an unconscious action.

Even after explaining the modus operandi of the divining rod, there are still those who believe that the rod moves because of some mystical force. As a last resort, I demonstrate the following trick and suggest you try it: Have someone hold his hands clenched together as in the photograph. Now take your right hand with your forefinger extended and begin circling your subject's hand at a rate of about two revolutions per second. A mysterious thing will begin to take place. Your subject's forefingers will appear to be drawn together as though some hidden force were causing the two fingers to be

attracted to each other. What is really the case is that even if you did
not circle his fingers with your forefinger, the fingers would be drawn
together because of the positioning of his hands. If his fingers do not
begin to move together, suggest to your friend that he relax his
fingers, and they will then begin to move toward each other.
Although this stunt does not cause the same muscular response as
the dowsing demonstration, it makes one point clear: One can bring
about undetected movements of an individual's hand without that
individual being aware of what is physically taking place.

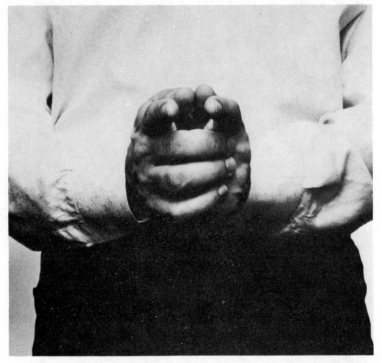

To illustrate "apparent control" over another person, try this trick. Have
someone hold his hands clenched together as in the photograph. Take your
right hand, with your forefinger extended, and circle your subject's hand in a
clockwise direction. His fingers will be drawn together as if by some unseen
force. However, even if you did not circle his fingers with your forefinger, his
fingers would be drawn together because of the position of his hands.

In the story aired, there was no attempt to scientifically prove the man's purported ability. There was only the stressing of the weird qualities of what he was doing, which, of course, made for an interesting report.

Dr. Koch's case leaves much to be desired. He assumes that something of the supernatural dimension had taken place by the statement of the Christian man. It appears that because of the man's prayer, water was not to be found. How do we know that the proclaimed dowser had an ability in the first place? Again an improper cause-and-effect relationship had been assumed. This is not an uncommon occurrence among well-meaning Christian people who do not have all the facts. I do not condone the practice of dowsing—not because a supernatural power is unleashed, but rather because it furthers superstitious thought.

There are those individuals, however, who do display an uncanny ability to discover water by means of dowsing. Mr. Rawcliffe, in his book *Occult and Supernatural Phenomena* points out, after exhaustive research, that there are subtle surface clues that may allow one to discern where underground streams or pockets of water may exist. The following is only a partial list of surface clues that may subconsciously aid the dowser: (1) naturally absorbant substratum and subsoil; (2) growth of vegetation; (3) temperature of surrounding air; (4) smell of damp earth; (5) underground streams audible to the ear; and (6) ground vibrations due to underground stream. It must be noted that most clues are very subtle and, for the most part, are registered subliminally by the dowser and then translated by ideomotor action into the dipping of the rod.

The only case that would cause one to raise an eyebrow is the ability of Major C. A. Pogson, who between 1925 and 1928 was able to find water where drilling experts had not. His accuracy was forty-seven out of forty-nine tries; and he demonstrated his ability at the request of the government of Bombay in "drought stricken areas of India." But, under scientific conditions, there has never been a convincing study to lead one to believe that dowsing is a gift.

Mr. Christopher states the following in his book:

P. A. Ongley reported in the *New Zealand Journal of Science and Technology*, in 1948, that fifty-eight dowsers participated in tests

devised to determine their ability to mark the same spots they had
indicated with their eyes open when their eyes were closed, to tell if
buried bottles containing water, and otherwise give evidence of their
purported powers. Their scores were on pure-chance levels.
Seventeen other diviners who specialize in diverse fields were
observed. As in the earlier experiments in France, seven illness
detectors found twenty-five diseases in a patient who doctors said was
healthy, and one diviner, whose eyes were bandaged, said the leg over
which he worked had varicose veins. Actually it was an artificial limb.[13]

If one could actually find water because of some power channeled
through a dowsing rod, then one should be able to have his ears
plugged, have a mask put over his face to eliminate the aid of the
faculty of scent, and be blindfolded to remove the possibility of visual
clues from the terrain. Only under these conditions could one say
that some power beyond the six senses is utilized in dowsing. If the
United States Army believed that dowsers could actually locate
mines, it would not have spent millions of dollars to develop
sophisticated equipment to do the job, and advertisements would
have appeared in the classified columns of local newspapers to enlist
qualified dowsers. Let us allow common sense to prevail. Yes, the
dowsing rod can be used as a tool of the devil—to show what lengths
man will go to believe his own folly.

Danny Korem

PSYCHIATRIC COMMENT

None of my friends expects me to be able to find water on their
land by dowsing. Therefore, if I pretended to be able to dowse, or
even believed I could, I might consciously or subconsciously cause
the dowsing rod to bend at a certain spot. What if my friends actually
dug there? If they didn't find water, they would laugh it off. They
wouldn't really expect me to be able to find water anyway. They
would forget it a few weeks later. But, actually, their chances of
finding water, if they dig deep enough, are pretty good. If they do hit
water (and chances are pretty good they will), they will
psychologically tend to want to falsely give me the credit, brag about
it with amazement to their friends, and never forget it.

The same principles apply when I (as a physician) predict the sex of an unborn child. By knowing certain medical factors (e.g., frequency of sex, pH of vaginal douches, and so forth), I could probably guess correctly 55 or 60 percent of the time. When I guess wrong, my friends even forget that I guessed. When I guess right, they remember. It's just human nature. Because of this common psychological phenomenon, much of what is incredible seems to be credible, even though it really isn't. Hence, most humans are naively superstitious. Others, in reaction to this type of ignorance, go foolishly to the opposite extreme and rule out the possibility of anything supernatural, including God's existence.

Paul Meier, M.D.

5
Table Tilting Set on an Even Keel

If you have ever wanted to create your own instant spook show when you are alone with a few friends and the wolves are howling and lightning is flashing through your windows, then table tilting is for you!

My first contact with this pseudo-spiritual phenomenon occurred when I was a student at Tulane University. My archery teacher, having heard of my mentalism act and my debunking of occultic phenomena, asked if I had ever witnessed table tilting. I told her that I had, but never saw a table in action doing its thing. She related to me that she and a couple of girl friends had actually been able to cause a table to rap out answers to questions they posed to the table. She believed that they had been able to contact some kind of spirit.

Upon questioning their technique, I discovered that they sat around the table with the palms of their hands lightly pressing on the table. After a question had been posed, the table, within a few seconds, would rap once for yes and twice for no. By rapping, she meant that the table levered itself up on two legs and then came back down to the floor. Having certain suspicions, I asked her if it was a card table they were using, and she answered in the affirmative. At that point the case—for me—was closed. When I told her what I believed caused the tilting, she said I was wrong. At the next class meeting, she told me I was right. Her table is now being used for more conventional purposes.

Dr. Koch makes a sincere effort at trying to discern what is the motivating force that causes a table to tilt and rap out answers. But his primary interest is whether table tilting could cause "psychic disturbances" and how to deal with those disorders.

A certain man was an active spiritist. For years he practiced "table-lifting" and considered this to be a way of communicating with the dead. He continued with his occult practices so intensively that psychic disturbances set in. The effects of his spiritistic interest also appeared in his children and grandchildren. His oldest son committed suicide. His next son suffered from a persecution mania. His oldest daughter ended up in an insane asylum. Another daughter suffered from Parkinson's disease. Among his grandchildren the same picture emerged. One of them was a schizophrenic. Another suffers from weak nerves and hypersensitivity, and yet another lives a dissolute life, and has given birth to an illegitimate child. The first of the man's great-grand-children is now a psychopath and a delinquent.[14]

A home-help in her thirties came for an interview. She complained of various emotional disturbances such as depression, boredom, suicidal thoughts, and blasphemous thoughts against God and Christ. She had fits of rage and a tendency to mania. When she heard people praying, she felt like running away, or would block her ears and close her eyes. In the presence of faithful Christians she was disgusted by everything and felt a repugnance to the Word of God. She felt an urge to break and tear up everything around her.

Externally she was well off. She lived abroad with her employer in comfortable circumstances. She had the opportunity of a promising marriage but did not know whether she ought to burden a partner with her depressive state. My first question, whether the emotional conflicts had been brought on by the question of marriage, she answered negatively. A few questions about previous ailments disclosed nothing more than a few colds. She had not reached the change of life. Next came the anamnesis of occult involvement. Her first reaction to my question about occult activity was one of ignorance. There was nothing to do but to go with her through the whole catalog of occult activities. She was surprised when I mentioned table-lifting. She admitted that she had done this for years, and saw nothing harmful in it. Her mistress had often taken her to a club where table-lifting was practiced amid solemn ceremonies. One day, as she faced a very weighty decision, it entered her mind to have a try at table-lifting in private. According to her report the experiment took place in the following way. The girl set a little parlour table in front of her, and used the same solemn phrase which she had heard at the club. But she could not remember the second phrase.

The little table remained motionless. She flung out a curse, "If you won't move in God's name, then move in the devil's name!" Thereupon the table began to tap. This was for this girl the beginning of years of habitual table-lifting. In answer to further questions, it became once again clearly established that for years she had practiced table-lifting in private; that she did not use her table for giving advice to other people, but that in every important question and decision she consulted it. To answer "yes" it would incline itself towards her; for "no", it would sway sideways. She never darkened her room during this practice.[15]

Dr. Koch further advances his own beliefs on the issue below.

The ultimate extreme of this phenomenon of table-lifting is reached in the verbal reports of researchers and missionaries from Tibet, who unanimously testify that many priests of the Tashi Lama possess enormous occult abilities and can make small tables fly through the air for a distance of a hundred feet. The so-called red-hooded monks are masters par excellence of telekinesis, levitation, materialization and black magic. It is not possible to check these fantastic reports by researchers from Tibet. The only argument for their probability and truthfulness is that these reports fit in with the general attitude to life in Tibet. For according to travelling researchers and missionaries, Tibet is of all countries and peoples of the world the greatest stronghold of occultism.[16]

Let me state more clearly why I have chosen to quote cases from the research of Dr. Koch. Many Christian bookstores have sprung up across the country in recent years. Many people who seek spiritual guidance go to these stores to purchase books on subjects about which they wish to become knowledgeable. It is unfortunate, but there has not risen to the surface one who is truly an expert on the discernment of occult versus pseudo-occult phenomena. One of the most widely read authors in this field because of his exhaustive research is Dr. Koch. Unfortunately, his background does not include a comprehensive study of legerdemain and he fails to enlist an individual with such a background to aid in his investigation.

There is a great tendency by many Christian authors to unintentionally sensationalize reports of purported occult phenomena and not to qualify these histories with the same rigidity trained physicians would use to record and diagnose their medical cases. This should be mandatory. Dr. Koch assumes, according to his writings, that such powers as telepathy, clairvoyance, and so forth, really exist. This is the base from which he works despite the fact that there has never been any conclusive evidence to give credence to this point of view. This, along with other gross misconceptions concerning the occult, could produce disastrous results if one is counseling a person with psychiatric disorders which the counselor believes are a direct result of some occultic-supernatural power. Mr. Christopher relates the following information concerning table tilting.

> Michael Faraday, the British physicist, ended scientific conjecture about table turning in 1853. He demonstrated dramatically that tables tilted or spun because people pushed them. He sandwiched pencil-thin glass rods between two small flat boards and held the rods in place by winding rubber bands around the boards. An indicator attached to the device revealed the slightest displacement of the upper surface. The device set on the table, the participant put his fingers on it rather than the wooden top. Each time the table moved, the indicator showed the top board had been moved in that direction. When the subjects were aware that the movements of their fingers were signaled, the table remained motionless. If the indicator was hidden from their view, pressures again were observed. It was proved that many people were not consciously aware that their hands had followed their thoughts.[17]

It is amazing that since 1853 the mystery of table tilting has been exposed, yet there are still countless books on the occult still being published which claim that table tilting is a psychic manifestation. The most common belief is that the participants are able to contact the spirits of the dead. In a later chapter it will be conclusively shown that the dead cannot make contact with the living. It should be obvious to the reader that table tilting is merely an outgrowth of ideomotor action.

One can now see why I am a strong believer in separating the wheat from the chaff where the supernatural is concerned. I do believe supernatural manifestations are possible, but I also believe that most phenomena are not borne in the supernatural but can be explained via natural causes. In the two cases Dr. Koch reported, there are no direct correlations between the table tilting and the psychological problems encountered. Table tilting cannot bring about Parkinson's disease, and neither can it cause an illegitimate birth, as hinted in the first case.

In the case of the home-help, the physical act of table tilting did not cause the woman's depressive state. It is more likely that her problem can be attributed to her desperate wanting for attention, as graphically illustrated by her cry, "If you won't move in God's name, then move in the devil's name." One might be inclined to point out that the devil moved the table as the table only moved after her calling to the devil. This is unlikely because of the direction of the movement of the table. The table tilted *towards* her to answer yes. Now if the table tilted *away* from her, the possibility of a supernatural movement may have existed.

To cause a table to tilt towards the subject, it is only necessary to apply a small amount of pressure on the edge of the table nearest the subject. Try it on a table in your home, and this will be made crystal clear. She stated that the table would sway back and forth when the answer is no. Again, this is very easy to accomplish when pressure is being applied to the edge of the table with an accompanying sideways movement of the hands. There existed an obvious hunger on this woman's part for spiritual direction.

If one accepts the premise of godly spiritual warfare versus the satanic, as outlined throughout the Bible, then one can see that Satan, at the time of the recording of Dr. Koch's case, was winning.

This is not because some supernatural power was manifested, but rather because the woman sought spiritual direction outside of the Lord.

To Dr. Koch's credit, he does point out that the mere perusal of apparent occult phenomena can be harmful. He also states that "about nine out of ten cases where people claim that they have had some experience of God or the miraculous are not genuine." But like most writers on the occult, Dr. Koch spends most of his time pointing out the spectacular cases, which may or may not have any validity in relationship to the supernatural manifestations, rather than putting these cases in proper perspective and stating that something of a supernatural origin may or may not be taking place.

In one of my first magic books, I learned how to apparently cause a small table to levitate by strapping a ruler to the underside of my forearm. Then, when I placed my hands upon the table, I would allow the ruler to go underneath the table's edge. To effect the apparent levitation of the table, I merely had to raise my hands, the table being supported by the ruler. I have caused more than one friend to take note of my apparent "miracle." Naturally, I tell them it is a trick. There are other methods even more baffling which are common knowledge to a trained magician. The only power a table has is the power *we* give it. This can either be by trickery or ideomotor action. Both thrive on the ignorance of man and his willingness to launch—without thought—into another level of paganistic belief.

Danny Korem

PSYCHIATRIC COMMENT

All I can say about Dr. Koch's first example (the habitual "table lifter" whose offspring had various emotional problems, supposedly as a result of practicing table lifting) is that psychotic parents tend to have psychotic children. If one identical twin develops schizophrenia, for example, the chances of the other identical twin also becoming schizophrenic, according to extensive research, are 91 percent. If one parent is schizophrenic, about 50 percent of the offspring will also eventually become schizophrenic, partially because of genetics and partially because of environmental factors. To assume that the table lifter's offspring became schizophrenic because of the table lifting borders on the ridiculous. The hundred-foot Tibetan "table fly" wasn't much more believable.

While I was completing my medical training at a major university, the chairman of the parapsychology department was asked to leave when it was discovered that he was falsifying the so-called "scientific data" on occultic phenomena in order to get more government funding to continue to support that department. Even in the field of medicine, many researchers (although a definite minority) have been caught falsifying their data, even though it cost human lives, in order to gain prominence and more government funding. The believability in any kind of research is in its repeatability. Can it be repeated over and over with the same results by other independent researchers who don't care how the results come out?

Paul Meier, M.D.

6
The Ouija Board—Spelling in Motion

As she is hunched over the table, a hopeful fear clouds her watching eyes. Her brother sits across from her. A board on which the alphabet is printed is laid out before him. As if in a trance, he glides his hands smoothly over its surface. They rest on the triangular planchette that indicates each letter selected. If it weren't for the morbid anticipation, one might think a child's parlor game were being played.

"Yes, he is alive," exclaims the male acting as the medium and interpreter of the simple board made of cardboard and paper. "He is living in Israel under an assumed name," the man positively states. "He is definitely alive."

This gruesome scene took place in my house when I was in high school. The participants, who will be nameless, were engaged in a very popular pseudo-occultic pastime, the Ouija board. The woman had not heard from her husband in several months, following a mysterious plane ride to Canada. It was known that her husband had engaged in illegal activities. The possibility of his being murdered was great. The brother, having had some luck with predicting future personal events by the laying of cards, decided to try his luck with the Ouija board. The anxiety created by the brother's statement was less than merciful. You see, the woman's husband was not found in Israel, but discovered several months later in a shallow grave in Canada with a bullet in his head.

Because the alphabet is laid out on the Ouija board, this seemingly harmless game can prove to be one of the most dangerous of the pseudo-occultic pursuits already detailed. With this "game," it is possible to create more illusionary answers of what the future may hold. It can also have a more devastating effect on those already unstable. Mr. Christopher relates in detail the morbid results of a paganistic belief in this oracle of folly:

> E. J. Turley, a former sailor who lived on a ranch in Arizona, was shot in the back with two bullets from a double-barreled shotgun. His teenage daughter, Mattie, explained that she had been walking behind him, had tripped, and the gun had fired as she fell. Investigation proved that the bullets would have been in alignment with the barrels of the weapon only if the fifteen-year-old girl had held it supported by her shoulder while in a standing position. Confronted by this scientific evidence, she told a different story to Justice of the Peace, Frank Whiting, and the local sheriff.

> Mattie said her mother had consulted an Ouija board to learn if she should stay with her husband or live with a romantic cowhand. The Ouija board offered a solution that terrified the child. She was told to kill her father.

> Her mother took the answer calmly and asked other questions as to how this should be carried out. A shotgun was indicated; five thousand dollars would be paid by her husband's insurance company and the law would not punish the girl for her action.

> Twice Mattie tried to carry out the instructions the Ouija board had given her; twice her finger on the trigger failed to pull at the crucial moment. The third time she fired. The "spirit advice" was wrong on two counts. Her mother did not get the insurance money, and the child did not escape legal consequences for the crime.[18]

We have seen how muscle reading, the pendulum, dowsing, and table tilting all operate due to ideomotor action. Throw in a little luck and coincidence, and a whole new realm of belief is created. The Ouija board is no different. From the historical account by Marcellinus to the encounter with the Ouija board of my two neighbors, the pursuit is the same: to discover what really took place in some elusive past event; and to learn what challenges the future will present. In Jastrow's experiments he showed that when a subject concentrates on an object with a degree of intensity, his hands and even his whole body will move in that direction. So it is true with the Ouija board.

Mr. Christopher relates that "Isaac Fuld, a cabinet maker who owned a small toy factory in Baltimore" patented his Ouija board in 1892. The name was derived from the French *oui* and the German *ja* which both mean "yes." Fuld admitted the motivating force that caused the planchette to move was "involuntary muscular actions," although he left open the possibility of spiritual intervention—to promote sales, no doubt—by adding the possibility that "some other agency" may cause the movement of the planchette. Many variations of the Ouija board have been experimented with by those who cater to the unknown, unseen, and the illogical. If my criticism seems a bit harsh, it is because of the ill effects that I have seen come about as the result of playing with such pseudo-psychic toys. Dr. Koch relates one such deviation from the original game.

At a Bible conference a Christian worker with university training related the following experience. His desire to investigate spiritualistic phenomenon led him to take part in séances. The members of the circle sat around a table upon which a large alphabet was spread out. The letters were covered with a sheet of glass, on which a liquor glass stood. After the séance had been opened with a philosophical religious prayer, a spirit was invoked. Those present directed questions to the invisibly present spirit, which were answered by the liquor glass dancing over the alphabet and coming to rest on single letters. When the letters were written down in order, they gave the answer to the question.

The narrator of the experience first of all took pains to determine what was the source of energy behind the individual movements of the glass, but his investigation, carried out at many séances, produced no result. Finally he found himself faced with the alternative of adopting the hypothesis either of actual spirits, or the much more readily understandable phenomenon of telekinesis (the ability to move objects by mere thought).[19]

Dr. Koch comments that what caused the glass to move "is only of secondary interest," and added that he was "concerned rather with the effects of this occult activity on the spiritual disposition of the experimenter."

When first reviewing a case, it should be determined if something of a supernatural took place and was manifested in the participants. If this is the case, then it should be dealt with from the supernatural realm, i.e. demon possession. If the occurrence was of the physical, i.e., trickery, ideomotor action, and so forth, it should be treated from an intellectual or psychiatric perspective.

The moving of the glass, in this case, was most assuredly brought about by trickery. This is a common magician's trick, and it has often been exposed.

The worker in question came to two conclusions: (1) Spirits of the deceased caused the movement of the glass (this is impossible and will be discussed later); (2) Telekinesis was the motivating force (this has never been proved, and in alleged "air-tight cases," a magician has always been able to unravel the true modus operandi).

By allowing this man to continue in these beliefs and not showing him what really happened, he will always live under the shadow of fear and doubt. This is particularly true if he was at all unstable or unsure of his beliefs before the séance. The reason Dr. Koch could not supply the needed answers is because he did not have the expertise necessary to unravel the mystery. The worker claimed to have observed carefully what might have caused the glass to move, but he is no match for a fraudulent psychic or spiritist who uses conjuring tricks to convince others of his ability to contact the dead or some advice-giving spirit.

I have never witnessed, read, or heard of a credible report of something of a supernatural nature taking place through the use of the Ouija board. I have seen, heard, and read, however, of many negative experiences that have entrapped people who have sought knowledge with a Ouija board. If you own a Ouija board or some similar diversion, my advice is to destroy it and never encourage others to tinker with such devices. You never know what emotional disturbances might be triggered in yourself or others through their use.

If you are still unconvinced and believe that some power might be manifested, then one should utilize the following procedure. The letters should be scattered at random, without your knowledge of their position, around the board; a bag should be placed over your head to prevent your viewing the board; and the entire letter-finding task should be viewed by a qualified magician, who would verify your lack of vision. Then and only then, if there are forces at work, will they produce something literate let alone prophetic. To save you the time and effort, let me add that this has already been tried with negative results.

Danny Korem

PSYCHIATRIC COMMENTS

I certainly agree with Danny Korem that any results obtained from Ouija boards is from either trickery, luck, or subconscious ideomotor action. I have had scores of psychiatric patients, both Christian and non-Christian, who have related incidents of Ouija-board usage. In none of these cases was there any evidence of demonic intervention. A few related having "bad luck" after Ouija board use, but every human I know had unwanted events happen in his life which seem like "bad luck," given enough time. There was no reason for me to assume naively that their bad luck has any direct correlation to their Ouija-board use.

Most of the patients I have had who used Ouija boards for personal direction were either: (1) very passive-dependent individuals, or else (2) borderline schizophrenics. In both types of individuals, I would expect a much greater incidence of supposed bad luck, since I believe most of us determine our own degree of good luck by personal responsibility and preparation.

I always encourage my patients to throw away their Ouija boards, if they mention them, for two basic reasons:

(1) God gave each of us a *brain* to think with and a *will* to make decisions with. To make passive decisions based on the luck of a Ouija-board game is absolutely stupid!

(2) The use of Ouija boards, or other objects usually associated with occultic or pseudo-occultic phenomena, is not only a poor testimony of one's character but also a bad example to our younger or more immature followers who may make passive and stupid life decisions based on trickery, luck, or subconscious ideomotor action.

Paul Meier, M.D.

7
Automatic Writing

This is by far the most complex phenomenon to unravel. Automatic writing is the apparent ability to write on subjects about which one has no knowledge. The subject goes into a trancelike state while a pencil is in hand and a sheet of paper is handy. While in this self-induced, trancelike state, the subject then details areas of knowledge totally foreign to that person's training and experience. Below is a case from Dr. Koch's writings:

A farmer's wife had a pain in her right forearm. At first the pain was treated as rheumatism but one day the woman made the interesting discovery that the pain would suddenly subside if she wrote a letter. Having discovered this, whenever the pain became unbearable she would always take a pencil and begin to write in order to alleviate the pain. But after a period of time the woman developed a writing compulsion. She would write things down that she could, normally speaking, never have written. Added to this, the written matter on each occasion turned out to be some form of religious treatise. The woman took the articles to her minister to let him examine them. He was surprised at their intellectual content, for the woman had had little or no formal education. By now the originally harmless activity had become a definite habit of automatic writing. One day the name Felix appeared in her notes. It was supposedly the name of a spirit who claimed that the woman had been chosen by God to pass on some special revelations to the world. He announced himself with the words, "In the name of the Lord Jesus, our blessed and exalted Lord and Savior," and had then gone on to say that she was to be a prophetess who would bless mankind through her writings. The simple farmer's wife had by now become a spiritistic writing medium.[20]

The ability to perform some task without devoting one's attention to it is a common occurrence. Tommy Martin, one of the two best magic acts during the days of vaudeville, told me that he learned his eight-minute act so well that at times he felt he could almost step out of his body and watch himself perform, without the effort of remembering what trick or beat of the music came next. At times I have caught myself practicing some new piece of sleight of hand, completely unaware of what I was doing until someone stopped and stared at my playing with a coin. Is it not possible then that a person could write without his attention being concentrated on what was being written?

Mr. Rawcliffe reports that Dr. Anita Muhl, in her 1930 treatise *Automatic Writing*, stated: "Given the right conditions," it was possible to train "normal, well-balanced individuals to write automatically." Continuing, he adds, "With her patients she used autonography to delve into their minds and resuscitate repressed memories and idea-associations."[21]

It is worth recording that one of Dr. Muhl's patients even wrote music autonographically. Others among her patients autonographically produced bizarre, cryptic, and sometimes beautifully colored drawings, whose symbolic content was resolved with the aid of subsequent automatic writings and which together formed the basis of the analytical therapy. There are also individuals who have dual personalities and assume the role of the other personality while they are writing.

It is apparent that automatic writing, or autonography, is an ability that can be developed. However, as mentioned in the previous sections, this ability could trigger latent or easily surfacing psychological trauma. The possibility of some outside force influencing such writings has never been conclusively proven. But due to the possibility of an eruption of a psychological disorder, the author does not—for any reason—recommend tampering with this pseudo-mystical phenomenon.

Danny Korem

PSYCHIATRIC COMMENT

Dr. Koch's example of the farmer's wife sounds similar to scores of psychiatric patients I have had. Patients who do so-called automatic writing of "messages from God," solutions to the world's problems, and so forth, are nearly always my manic-depressive or schizophrenic patients. In both types, the individual feels so inferior in the real world that when he becomes psychotic (out of touch with reality), he develops *delusions of grandeur* (thinking he is great or has special psychic powers) in order to compensate for his true severe feelings of insignificance. In their psychotic state, they sit down and write whatever will make them feel superior, intellectual, and powerful. They use big words that they would normally never use in their vocabulary, words they remember hearing. They often use these big words incorrectly. Then they sometimes convince themselves that they didn't really write this great treatise under their own power, but rather under the inspiration of God, which makes them feel significant. They are so psychotic that convincing themselves of such things is easy. I know of one patient (during my psychiatric training at Duke University Medical Center) who spent hours each day riding up and down an elevator, pushing all the buttons, then commanding in the name of the Lord that the elevator doors open and shut at each floor. He was convinced that the doors opened and shut because of his spiritual powers, while instantly repressing the fact that he had just pushed all the elevator buttons.

From my experience, so-called automatic writing is usually a similar phenomenon, especially when the result is some pseudo-intellectual treatise on the world's problems with religious solutions to those problems. I would treat any patient having this type of experience with antipsychotic medications and psychotherapy aimed at improving their self-concepts. The "automatic" writing ability always goes away after a week or two of antipsychotic medication and ego-building, supportive, reality-oriented counseling.

Now, the other related, milder phenomena that Danny Korem discusses, like automatic doodling, are nothing to worry about. Almost every normal person I know will do some degree of automatic doodling while listening to a lecture or sermon, especially when bored. Only about 20 percent of our thoughts are conscious, with the other 80 percent being subconscious or unconscious. The doodles one draws semiautomatically, while trying to concentrate on a boring sermon, are very revealing to a psychiatrist. All humans have unconscious conflicts that are being thought of unconsciously during nearly every waking moment and even during dreams at night. A person with repressed sexual conflicts, for example, will frequently be surprised when he looks down at his church bulletin during a boring sermon and finds that most of his doodles are shaped like genitalia. He rapidly joins the doodles together so they look like a cobweb or something else and he may even deny to his conscious awareness the fact that they really did look like the genitalia of the opposite sex. This type of phenomenon is very common—almost universal—and is, in my opinion, more amusing than worrisome. It can also be insightful. But I would agree with Danny Korem that the more complex "automatic" writing itself should not be sought after, because it could trigger psychological disturbances.

Paul Meier, M.D.

8

Psychic Surgery: The Hands Are Quicker Than the Blade—Or a Cut Below the Norm

I once witnessed a television documentary that dealt with different types of mysterious phenomena. One area that was covered and supposedly validated by rare film footage, was what has become known as *psychic surgery*. The clip showed a patient stretched out on a bed, and a man madly working to heal some abdominal ailment. Triumphantly, the psychic surgeon held up some bloody goo and stated that the operation was a success. The host of the documentary stated that the "healing" caused by psychic means did not even leave a scar. Dr. Koch relates the following story.

I came across the story of an "astral surgeon" in the Philippines. Spiritists believe, that as well as having a material body, man also possesses an astral body. This particular man, it was claimed, was able to do operations on the astral bodies of people. Without the use of any instruments he merely manipulated with his hands above the person's body. The whole idea seems at first sight ridiculous, but let us have a look at the results of such operations.

One woman, who was known through X rays to be suffering from gallstones, went and visited this astral surgeon. Subsequently new X rays showed that the stones had disappeared. It was a case of some sort of spiritistic apport, an apport being the appearance or disappearance of an object within a closed space. It may perhaps also have been an example of dematerialization, where a substance just disintegrates and dissolves into nothing.[22]

And what follows is an even more amusing story which is related in Tim Timmons's *Chains of the Spirit*. You will understand why I use *amusing*, in the commentary that follows this next "case" of psychic surgery.

Through the deception of the occult, false teachers may receive occult powers unknowingly, believing these powers are the supernatural gift of God. This is obvious in the astounding case of a Mexican peasant woman I interviewed, whom I will call Carlita. Carlita first noticed she possessed healing power when she was able to cure animal diseases in the circus where she had worked all her life. This continued for some time until one afternoon a spirit by the name of Hermanito Cuauhtemoc came upon her. He explained to Carlita that he was sent by God to heal people through her. She accepted the opportunity to be used by God in this way; and Cuauhtemoc has now been healing people through Carlita for nearly fifty years.

Carlita's healings are strange! She does not pray over a person asking God to heal them—she actually operates on people with a dull hunting knife! Over the past fifty years, she has performed every kind of operation imaginable—on the heart, the back, the eyes, etc. A medical doctor who had observed Carlita perform many operations was present when I interviewed her. He told of one case where Carlita cut into a person's chest cavity, took the heart out for examination, and handed it to him. After she closed the person up, without stitches, she suggested that he go to his hotel room and rest for three days. When the three days were up, he left Mexico City, a healthy man, with no scars from surgery. I asked the doctor what explanation he could give for such an amazing work. He replied, "There is no explanation medically. It's a miracle."

The remarkable thing about Carlita's work is that she always operates in a dark room with her eyes shut. The reason for this is that Carlita does not do the operation herself—Hermanito Cuauhtemoc acts through her. When he takes over her body, her eyes close and he speaks and acts through her—he has total control.

One intelligent, mature man from the United States was skeptical when he went to view an operation for the second time. Cuauhtemoc sensed that the man did not believe, so he took the man's hand on the operating table and made him take out a tumor that was in the person's back. This man is no longer a skeptic! He told me, "I don't care if it is God's power or Satan's, because it is real and people are being helped through it."

Carlita's ministry comes from a sincere heart; she gives all of the glory to God who she believes sent Cuauhtemoc to work these mighty acts of power through her. Nevertheless, she is being deceived. Carlita is a medium by her own admission, and it is Cuauhtemoc who is in control, not the Lord. He claims to be the spirit of the ancient Aztec Indian Chief who is now chief of all the spirits in North America. He was sent by his "god" all right—Satan, the god of this world. Carlita is deceived by the false belief that everything supernatural must be from God, especially if it helps people. After talking with Carlita for two hours, and listening to Cuauhtemoc twice during the evening, I asked her the source of her power. She answered, "If not God, who else?"[23]

My good friend, Andre Kole, was sent on assignment by *Time* magazine to the Philippines to investigate claims of miraculous healings. Andre is one of the world's most creative illusionists. He practices that part of the art of legerdemain where he apparently levitates people, saws women in half, and performs fantastic feats on the stage. He has spent tens of thousands of dollars to produce the finest illusions in the world. To date, he has performed live for over 53 million people in more than sixty foreign countries. He can be considered an expert in his field. On this trip to the Philippines he exploded the myth of the psychic surgeons by exposing their use of both simple and well-known conjuring props to perpetuate their frauds.

There is a magic trick sold in a few of the better shops where one is able to create the illusion of a hat pin going through the center of one's forearm. The effect is so realistic, as blood appears to flow from the wound, that I have seen grown men faint. The photograph shows why one would think that this sharp instrument is actually penetrating the arm.

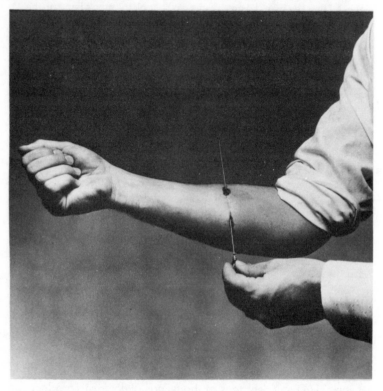

Shown here is a demonstration of apparent injury and instantaneous healing of the body. A hat pin is seemingly pushed through the arm, which appears to bleed. When the pin is removed and the arm wiped off, not so much as a puncture mark is to be found. The trick is merely an illusion made possible by a magician's prop.

Another trick which I found in an old book on conjuring is equally as effective in appearance. I have used it on occasion as a party stunt. Very carefully, I would take a butcher's knife—the bigger the better as far as theatrical effect is concerned—and draw it across my thumb. Immediately blood would appear where the apparent wound had been opened. Then taking my "magic Band-aid," a piece of a cotton ball, I touched it to the wound and wonder of wonders, the cut was "healed"! This is one of the few tricks I will disclose but perhaps few will want to go through the pain of presenting it. For those who do, here it is:

Clean the top of your thumb behind the nail with some alcohol. Now take a sterilized sewing needle and lightly jab it into the skin just behind the nail. (I didn't say that this would be enjoyable!) If you apply pressure with the forefinger of the same hand to the flesh part of the thumb, blood will issue forth. This is how the trick works. Just before you are ready to present this feat, secretly prick your skin so that blood will come forth when pressure is applied to the thumb. Then, with your other hand, take the butcher's knife and lightly draw it across the pin-pricked area. Take care that you do not cut yourself or the trick won't work, and neither will your thumb! As you draw the blade across the thumb, your forefinger applies pressure causing blood to come forth from the pin prick. As the blade continues moving across the thumb, it will pull the blood along with it giving the appearance that you are cutting your thumb. What the spectator sees is merely a fine line of blood "drawn" by the blade of the knife. To "heal" the wound merely wipe the blood with a cloth.

I have followed up this trick by palming a carrot and apparently covering my thumb but really covering the carrot. With a few quick jabs of the knife, it appears that you are really stabbing your thumb. The crunching sound of the knife going into the carrot is my favorite part. To complete the gag, I reveal the carrot and let my slightly nauseated viewers have a good laugh on themselves. Naturally I let my unsuspecting victims know that everything they have witnessed is a trick.

The purpose of this explanation is not to provide you with a trick which will amaze your friends, but rather to give you the feeling of how the psychic surgeon operates. I cannot reveal the actual gimmicks he might use because some are employed by professional

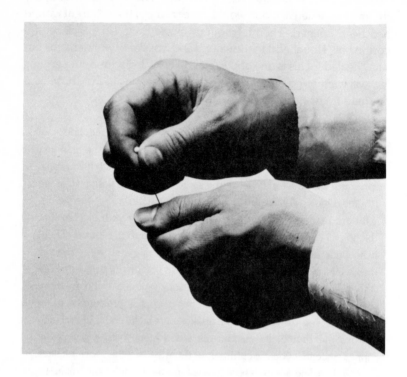

These photos illustrate one type of deception used by fraudulent "psychic surgeons." First, a small pin prick is made behind the nail of the thumb.

magicians in their shows. By these gimmicked means, one can cause the appearance of blood, remove a decayed chicken liver, and pass it off for some part of the anatomy. A good physician could easily examine the substance and reach the conclusion that the extracted part did not come from a human, but then no doctor in his right mind would pursue such a ridiculous avenue of treatment.

Dr. Koch's case story is just another example of inaccurate analysis as a result of some misconceptions. He never witnessed what happened and admits that he "came across the story." He then states—hypothetically—that this phenomenon may be due to some "spiritistic apport," and he grasps for answers by stating that this

As the knife is pulled across the thumb, the forefinger exerts pressure on the thumb, causing a small drop of blood to come up through the pin prick. The blood follows the blade of the knife and makes it appear that the thumb is actually being cut.

may be an example of dematerialization. Perhaps he has watched too many Buck Rogers' films. Concerning the disappearance of the gallstones, Dr. Koch does not state who took the X rays. Very likely they were taken by a cohort of the mock surgeon. It is possible that the individual in question might have imagined some sort of gallbladder disorder and when she was convinced that she was healed, the symptoms went away.

Mr. Timmon's story is one of the funniest accounts of some one being duped that I have encountered. In defense of Mr. Timmons, it

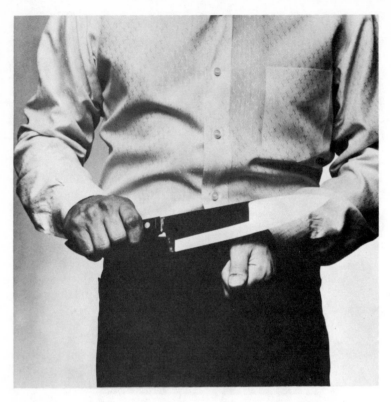

When the blood is wiped from the thumb, it appears the cut has instantaneously healed.

should be stated that he has written some excellent books on Christian counseling and that he is a graduate of Dallas Theological Seminary where Dr. Meier is a professor. Because one is knowledgeable in one field, however, does not necessarily mean one is qualified to be an authority in another. This is a mistaken mind-set that often prevails in our country. I am not belittling the academic community, as evidenced by my seeking the assistance of Dr. Meier and Mr. Lundeen, but I think one should temper one's opinion of an authoritative source, considering the expertise of that individual. Mr. Timmons's or Dr. Koch's expertise is not in the field of legerdemain, and their writings in this area should be considered in light of this fact.

Carlita was very shrewd in having a physician give credence to her powers. Whether he was duped or participated in the sham is unclear. What is amusing is that she only performs her "surgery" in the dark. Of course, with few conjuring techniques at her disposal, how else could she convince her takers that she removed someone's heart with a dull hunting knife! The statement that the wound healed without scarring in three weeks is also easily explained. A slight cutting of the skin where the operaration supposedly took place would heal without a scar. The cut actually gave the "surgery" some validity. The apparent healing again cannot be verified as being imaginary or psychosomatic. Is it not obvious why the psychic surgeons couldn't make the first cut for the American Medical Association?

Danny Korem

PSYCHIATRIC COMMENT

The psychic-surgery story at the beginning of this chapter is incredible. Even if the patient did have gallstones that showed on X ray, they could easily have been dissolved or been passed out of the gallbladder. The patient was more likely a hysterical personality who was duped into believing she had gallstones in the first place.

I have had literally hundreds of patients, including some registered nurses, who thought they had all sorts of actual physical ailments. On occasion, I have given them a simple saline (saltwater) injection and they falsely assumed that I was giving them some powerful medicine. In nearly every case, the gallbladder or other imagined symptoms went away within twenty minutes. Since I don't believe in lying, I always tell the patient that they really received no medicine at all, and that their symptoms were tricks played by their minds. I do this to prove the truth to them. With a few lessons in psychic surgery from Danny Korem, along with my psychiatric training, I am sure I could become a famous "psychic surgeon" overnight.

Paul Meier, M.D.

9
Fire Walkers: Men on the Move

No one forgets the sensation of being burned. It is the memory of this never-to-be-forgotten ordeal that makes fire walkers so effective at suspending the belief of the observer. Why can one person walk across fiery beds of coals and stones and another cannot? What the fire walker has going for him is that few people will go to the trouble to find the answer.

Fire walking has been practiced for several thousand years. Deuteronomy 18:10 warns the Israelites from causing their sons or daughters to pass "through the fire." Fire walking has been practiced in Japan, the Fiji Islands, India, the northern and southern parts of Africa, and India, where it is most popularly known. Vergil, Strabo, and Pliny all give accounts of this feat taking place in Cappadocia two thousand years ago. Do not confuse this phenomenon with the following account in the Book of Daniel, 3:14–26:

> Nebuchadnezzar spake and said unto them, Is it true O Shadrach, Meshach, and Abednego, do not ye serve my gods, nor worship the golden image which I have set up? Now if ye be ready that at what time ye hear the sound of the cornet, flute, harp, sackbut, psaltery, and dulcimer, and all kinds of musick, ye fall down and worship the image which I have made; well: but if ye worship not, ye shall be cast the same hour into the midst of a burning fiery furnace; and who is that God that shall deliver you out of my hands? Shadrach, Meshach, and Abednego, answered and said to the king, O Nebuchadnezzar, we are not careful to answer thee in this matter. If it be so, our God whom we serve is able to deliver us from the the burning fiery furnace, and he

will deliver us out of thine hand, O king. But if not, be it known unto thee, O king, that we will not serve thy gods, nor worship the golden image which thou hast set up. Then was Nebuchadnezzar full of fury, and the form of his visage was changed against Shadrach, Meshach, . . and Abednego: Therefore he spake, and commanded that they should heat the furnace one seven times more than it was wont to be heated. And he commanded the most mighty men that were in his army to bind Shadrach, Meshach, and Abednego, and to cast them into the burning fiery furnace. Then these men were bound in their coats, their hosen, and their hats, and their other garments, and were cast into the midst of the burning fiery furnace. Therefore because the king's commandment was urgent, and the furnace exceeding hot, the flame of the fire slew those men that took up Shadrach, Meshach, and Abednego. And these three men, Shadrach, Meshach, and Abednego, fell down bound into the midst of the burning fiery furnace. Then Nebuchadnezzar the king was astonied, and rose up in haste, and said unto his counsellors, Did not we cast three men bound into the midst of the fire? They answered and said unto the king, True, O king. He answered and said, Lo, I see four men loose, walking in the midst of the fire, and they have no hurt; and the form of the fourth is like the Son of God. Then Nebuchadnezzar came near to the mouth of the burning fiery furnace, and spake, and said, Shadrach, Meshach, and Abednego, ye servants of the most high God, come forth, and come hither. Then Shadrach, Meshach, and Abednego, came forth of the midst of the fire.

Let it be noted that in the biblical text, the three men were to be executed. They were not going to present a demonstration of fire walking as is commonly observed. Incidentally, fire walking is not the passing through flaming fires. What actually takes place is that the participants walk across a bed of coals or heated stones, not a leaping bonfire as some might think. In verses 21-23, the text states that the three men were wearing their hosen (socks). No fire walker in his right mind would step across coals let alone be exposed to flames with socks on his feet. The material would instantly catch fire. It is also stated that the three men, after being bound and tossed into the flames, fell down in the midst of the furnace. Few fire walkers would risk more than a few steps across a hot bed of coals. Let it also be noted that the men who threw Shadrach, Meshach, and Abednego into the furnace were consumed by the "flame of the fire," which makes it plain that the three men were indeed cast into a flaming furnace and not into a furnace that was merely heated coals or stones. This is an important point that will later be pursued.

Fire walking, as presented today, does not meet the same criteria. As mentioned earlier, fire walking is really walking on hot coals or stones. Fire walking was brought to the limelight in this country by the well-known magician Kuda Bux, from Kashmir, Pakistan. He is a former resident magician of the famed Magic Castle in Los Angeles, where I have also had the honor of performing and lecturing.

In 1935, Harry Price, one of the best-known psychic researchers in England, set up a trench of hot coals twenty feet long, several inches thick, with a surface temperature of 430 degrees centigrade (806 degrees Fahrenheit), with the interior temperatures reaching 1,400 degrees centigrade (2,552 degrees Fahrenheit). Kuda, without the aid of ointments or chemicals being applied to his bare feet, taking four strides in 4.5 seconds, crossed the pit four times without the slightest trace of his skin being burned or blistered.

Before I go further, let me also tell you about another trick Kuda has perfected. His blindfold act is the best in the business. Volunteers from the audience pack dough over his eyes and cover them with adhesive bandages. Then Kuda's entire head is encircled with many feet of heavy, thick linen. Although his vision is seemingly impaired, he is able to see as if nothing is hindering his sight. I have watched him shoot the flame out of lighted candles at thirty feet with a .22-caliber rifle while in this state. Another demonstration involves a spectator holding a credit card, and after his hands hover above the card without touching it, he will tell you the number printed on it. There are others in our trade who can do this trick, but none can do it like Kuda. I can assure you of one thing: Kuda is a perfectionist and will never leave open the possibility of failure. And this applies to his famous walk.

It is common knowledge among magicians that one's hand can be placed in a vat of molten lead and removed without losing it in the process. This may not seem important to you, but it is to the one with his hands in the vat! This type of demonstration was recently presented on a national television show. A gentleman allowed molten aluminum alloy to be poured over his fingers without burning his hand in the process. This type of stunt relies upon short contact with the molten substance. It is the same idea as passing one's hand over a lit match or extinguishing a candle with one's fingers. It is the brevity of contact that prevents one from being burned. In some cases it is the moisture given off by the hands that creates a temporary insulating barrier. It is not advisable that you melt down a bar of lead and try your luck.

Another fakir stunt is the licking of a red-hot poker. As long as there is a little saliva on one's tongue, which adds to the effectiveness of the stunt as it sizzles, the tongue will not be burned as the poker is stroked along the tongue. As long as one maintains an even, yet brisk walk across a bed of coals, one will not be burned. This is the secret of this great trick.

It has been found that one cannot take more than four steps across a bed of coals without running the risk of being burned. In 1937, Ahmed Hussain, another coal walker, took six steps in 2.3 seconds to cross a twenty-foot pit (temperature 740 degrees Celsius) and was severely burned. There have been other laymen, however, who have successfully duplicated the coal-walking stunt. Walking on heated stones is even easier, since stone is a poor conductor of heat. You will not, however, witness a fakir walk across a heated steel plate, as steel is an excellent conductor of heat.

For centuries, fire walking has been practiced as a purification rite and as a spring fertility ritual. Both are pagan practices. That is why this ancient practice is disdained by Scripture. It was not declared taboo because a demon gave a participant some supernatural power, but rather because it aided Satan's cause in driving the Lord's chosen people from Him.

Danny Korem

PSYCHIATRIC COMMENT

We humans are so gullible and want so badly to believe the unbelievable that we don't even stop to ask ourselves healthy, skeptical questions. For example, why don't big-name faith healers ever heal a withered arm, like Jesus did? Or restore an ear that had been cut off, like Jesus did? Why don't Ouija-board "readers" use blindfolds? Why do psychic surgeons do their work in the dark? Why don't fire walkers walk within a hot furnace of flames like Shadrach, Meshach, and Abednego? Why do they walk on a twenty-foot bed of stones or coals in three or four quick steps? It's so obvious, and yet we tend to deny the obvious for various psychological reasons. The superstitiousness of Christians and those from unchurched backgrounds has not changed significantly since the Dark Ages. We have been duped over and over and over again, and we hate to admit it.

Paul Meier, M.D.

10
The Fraud of Endor

Death is the final and most powerful event in one's life that cannot be controlled. If one is a Christian, there is the hope of eternal life. For the nonbeliever, however, there is only a ghastly and hollow fear of that mysterious and seemingly cold and indifferent event that terminates one's physical life.

Shamans and witch doctors have, for thousands of years, claimed the ability to communicate with the spirits of the dead. As the centuries rolled along, man's gullibility continued. In the middle 1800s, spiritualism became the vogue which still persists today. Spiritualism is the belief that departed spirits are able to communicate with the living, usually through a medium. This so-called communication is carried out by rapping tables (table tilting), movements of the planchette on the Ouija board, or trances where the "spirit speaks" through a medium who purportedly has the ability to contact the dead. Spiritualism came into its own with the fraudulent Fox sisters.

The main story of spiritualism dates from 1848, when curious raps occurred in the presence of the Fox family of Rochester, New York. The pattern of these raps betrayed an intelligent source, said to be a murdered peddler. The two principals in this tableau were the Fox sisters, who were feted and encouraged to demonstrate their abilities in less parochial surroundings. This they did. One of them later recanted, and stated that she had made noises by voluntarily cracking her knee joints.[24]

Although there has never been an authenticated case which proved beyond a reasonable doubt that the spirits of the deceased can be contacted, millions believe that this is possible. Some will even go to the "Sister Ruths" to receive consolation from their departed ones and to gain a glimpse of the "other side." What is truly amazing is that some Christians will hold to these same paganistic beliefs.

In this section I will primarily address myself to those Christians who believe one can contact the spirit of one who is deceased. In all of Scripture there is only one report of a medium seemingly making contact with a spirit. The word *seemingly* is used because it will become clear that contact was never made with a departed spirit. The passage of Scripture is from 1 Samuel, 28:1-14, where the Philistines assemble against Israel:

> And it came to pass in those days, that the Philistines gathered their armies together for warfare, to fight with Israel. And Achish said unto David, Know thou assuredly that thou shalt go out with me to battle, thou and thy men. And David said to Achish, Surely thou shalt know what thy servant can do. And Achish said to David, Therefore will I make thee keeper of mine head for ever. Now Samuel was dead, and all Israel had lamented him, and buried him in Ramah, even in his own city. And Saul had put away those that had familiar spirits, and the wizards, out of the land. And the Philistines gathered themselves together, and came and pitched in Shunem: and Saul gathered all Israel together, and they pitched in Gilboa. And when Saul saw the host of the Philistines, he was afraid, and his heart greatly trembled. And when Saul enquired of the Lord, the Lord answered him not, neither by dreams, nor by Urim, nor by prophets. Then said Saul unto his servants, Seek me a woman that hath a familiar spirit, that I may go to her, and enquire of her. And his servants said to him, Behold, there is a woman that hath a familiar spirit at Endor. And Saul disguised himself, and put on other raiment, and he went, and two men with him, and they came to the woman by night: and he said, I pray thee, divine unto me by the familiar spirit, and bring me him up, whom I shall name unto thee. And the woman said unto him, Behold, thou knowest what Saul hath done, how he hath cut off those that have familiar spirits, and the wizards, out of the land: wherefore then layest thou a snare for

my life, to cause me to die? And Saul sware to her by the Lord, saying, As the Lord liveth, there shall no punishment happen to thee for this thing. Then said the woman, Whom shall I bring up unto thee? And he said, Bring me up Samuel. And when the woman saw Samuel, she cried with a loud voice: and the woman spake to Saul, saying, Why hast thou deceived me? for thou art Saul. And the king said unto her, Be not afraid: for what sawest thou? And the woman said unto Saul, I saw gods ascending out of the earth. And he said unto her, What form is he of? And she said, An old man cometh up; and he is covered with a mantle. And Saul perceived that it was Samuel, and he stooped with his face to the ground, and bowed himself.

What follows appears to be a dialogue between Saul and Samuel's spirit during which some startling "prophecies" are divined. This passage of Scripture has been used more than any other to prove that it is possible to make contact with spirits of the dead. Without doing any further research, it would be easy to understand why one might believe this to be true. Before we deal with the exposé, we need to first examine the circumstances surrounding Saul before his meeting with the alleged medium of Endor.

Saul was ceremonially anointed with oil by Samuel to symbolize that he was the one chosen to be king over Israel. The Lord removed His divine hand from Saul, however, when he disobeyed the Lord's command to slay the murderous Amalekites (1 Samuel 15:8-11). Because of Saul's disobedience, David was anointed by Samuel to be king. Saul realized this and tried to kill David on several occasions. David finally fled to the land of the Philistines. It was during David's exile that Samuel died. In reaction to Samuel's death, Saul "had put away those that had familiar spirits, and the wizards, out of the land" (1 Samuel 28:3). At the same time the Philistines were ready to attack, and Saul was afraid because "when Saul inquired of the Lord, the Lord answered him not . . ." (1 Samuel 28:6). Guilt and fear plagued heavily on Saul's mind, so he requested his servants to ". . . Seek me a woman that hath a familiar spirit, that I may go to her, and inquire of her" (1 Samuel 28:7).

After reading the verses that then ensue, one might come to the conclusion that when Saul met up with the purported medium, contact was established with Samuel. With careful scrutiny, we will discover what really happened.

In order to get the full flavoring of the Scripture we will examine the original Hebrew text. Some startling facts will come to light. Scholars of the Scriptures utilize two proven source books. One is called a concordance and the other is called a lexicon. The concordance lists every word that is contained in the Bible and the verses where it is used. The lexicon takes each Greek or Hebrew word from which the original texts were translated and shows the derivation of each word, how it was used, and how it came into being. Unfortunately, when literally translating any foreign language into our own language, it is difficult to capture the precise and exact meaning of specific words. This will be readily apparent when we see what the Hebrew word for "one that hath a familiar spirit" really meant to the Hebrew of that day. Whenever one pursues key doctrinal questions, one must always rely on the original Greek and Hebrew text to prevent unintentional misinterpretation of the Scriptures. Before getting into the nitty-gritty of the derivation and meaning of certain questionable words, let us take a look at how Saul was set up.

When Saul's servants informed him of the purported medium in Endor, the passage reads, "And Saul disguised himself, and put on other raiment . . . (1 Samuel 28:8). This very action on Saul's part was highly comical. Even if he could disguise his facial features, he could not disguise his height. First Samuel 9:2 tells us that Saul "from his shoulders and upward was taller than any of the people." This means that he was probably about seven feet tall. Unless he walked on his knees, anyone would know immediately who he was—especially the fraud of Endor!

The first request that he made of her was to bring forth the spirit of his choice. Her sly reply is, "Behold, thou knowest what Saul hath done, how he hath cut off those that have familiar spirits, and the wizards, out of the land: wherefore then layest thou a snare for my life, to cause me to die?" (1 Samuel 28:9).

Saul then swears to her that no harm shall come to her. Logically, it wouldn't take a highly trained mind to perceive, based upon Saul's oath that the disguised personage was Saul. Only the king could make such a promise *and* back it up. Her suspicion is confirmed when he asks her to raise up Samuel the prophet. Who else in all of Israel, who was seven feet tall, could back the requested oath and want to speak to Samuel? (In the next section of the book we will deal with the techniques utilized by fortune-tellers to *seemingly* discern hidden facts and events of their all-too-believing clientele.) In this case it is obvious that she was aware she was speaking to Saul even though he never told her.

As soon as he says, "Samuel," she lets out a scream. Scripture says she screamed when she saw Samuel, but as will later be detailed, it was *not* the popular belief of the day that one could communicate with spirits, and the reader of *that day* understood the *context* in which this statement was made. She then locks her hunch in solid by asking Saul why he has deceived her.

Saul assures her and then asks her whom she saw. Please note that neither Saul nor his servants saw anything. Only the *woman claims* to have seen something. The literal translation of what she claims to have seen is not "gods ascending out of the earth," but "the seed of God ascending out of the earth," which of course refers to Samuel. It is obvious whom she is referring to, but not to Saul. He asks for a description of this mystical spirit, and she tells him that "he is covered with a robe." It is amusing that she did not describe some hidden birthmark or physical quality of Samuel. She merely states that he had on a robe. What prophet of Israel didn't wear a robe? Because of this "miraculous" revelation, Saul concludes that the fraud of Endor has seen Samuel, and he immediately prostrates himself on the ground. It is *only* while Saul is so positioned that Samuel apparently speaks. Before going further let us examine a few critical words.

The first word is the Hebrew word, 'ôwb, which is pronounced *obe*. It is translated in the King James Version as "one that hath a familiar spirit." Other translations merely state a medium. Due to the translation, one might mistakenly think that this individual has the ability to call up a spirit with which she was familiar. This is far from the truth. The word 'ôwb was used to denote: (1) one who mumbles; (2) a skin bottle (water skin bottle used to hold water); (3) a hollow sound emitted by thumping; (4) one who mutters or speaks from the hollow of his belly, i.e. ventriloquist, as utilized in the practice of seeking instruction from the dead; (5) a necromancer or wizard; (6) possibly a ghost or spirit conceived as dwelling in necromancer. (But this was *not* the ancient conception.) The *Davis Dictionary of the Bible* states (p. 240, 1973 ed., Royal Pubs. Inc.), "The voice of the spirit which appeared to come from the ground emanated from the human pretender himself."

Samuel never spoke. The woman, through *ventriloquism* spoke in a deep, hollow-sounding voice. The Hebrew of that day *did not* believe that spirits could be contacted. A logical question then is why did Saul cast out all the mediums and wizards? History has demonstrated many times that when confronted with a great crisis people turn to something outside of the physical realm for answers. If they don't turn to God, they turn to any other available source that can give them an apparently supernatural answer. The rise in sales of the Ouija board during World War I is a case in point. Saul knew the Lord wasn't going to answer his prayers so he didn't want anyone else with purported contacts with the spirit world spreading alarm about what the people should or should not do. There is more hard evidence, however, that the woman at Endor was a fraud.

The Hebrew word for wizard is *yidd-oni'y*, pronounced *yid-deh-o-nee*. The Hebrew did not look at the wizard as one who had mystical powers but rather as one who *pretends* to have great knowledge and the ability to converse with the spirits of the dead. Isaiah properly referred to these purported mediums and wizards when he said, "And when they shall say unto you, Seek unto them that have familiar spirits, and unto wizards that peep, and that mutter: should not a people seek unto their God? .. (Isaiah 8:19). The "wizards and ones that have familiar spirits" are always mentioned together. The Hebrew use of the conjunction *and* in this passage denotes that the nouns so joined are equal. Therefore, if wizards are frauds, then so are the mediums or "those that have familiar spirits."

The reason Leviticus 20:27 states that these culprits are to be punished by death was not because of some supernatural power that they possessed, but rather because they furthered idolatry and paganistic thought. Unfortunately, Saul was looking for a quick way out, and the fraud of Endor provided such a path. It was a path leading out of the world of the living.

We must now deal with the seemingly incredible predictions the medium made concerning the future of Saul and his sons. It wouldn't take a purported clairvoyant long to recognize that the Lord had deserted Saul. Knowledge of Saul's transgressions were common knowledge as they were done out in the open. Historically, whenever the Lord removes His divine protection from an Old Testament figure, destruction always ensues. Listen to the dialogue from the medium.

> And Samuel said to Saul, Why hast thou disquieted me, to bring me up? And Saul answered, I am sore distressed; for the Philistines make war against me, and God is departed from me, and answereth me no more, neither by prophets, nor by dreams: therefore I have called thee, that thou mayest make known unto me what I shall do. Then said Samuel, Wherefore then dost thou ask of me, seeing the Lord is departed from thee, and is become thine enemy? And the Lord hath done to him, as he spake by me: for the Lord hath rent the kingdom out of thine hand, and given it to thy neighbor, even to David: Because thou obeyedst not the voice of the Lord, nor executedst his fierce wrath upon Amalek, therefore hath the Lord done this thing unto thee this day. Moreover the Lord will also deliver Israel with thee into the hand of the Philistines: and to morrow shalt thou and thy sons be with me: the Lord also shall deliver the host of Israel into the hand of the Philistines.
>
> 1 Samuel 28:15–19

It was not hard to predict that Saul and his sons would be slain in battle the next day, as the Lord was not with Saul, and he was afraid. Without leadership from the Lord and fearless leadership from the head of the armed forces, anyone could easily predict defeat. First Samuel 31:1 states that the "men of Israel fled from before the Philistines." In the pursuit, Saul's sons were slain, as they were a primary target of the Philistines. Saul, however, was only wounded. His overwhelming guilt and fear unleashed latent suicidal tendencies, and he tried to commit suicide by falling on his sword (1 Samuel 31:4), thus attempting to fulfill the prediction. Not finishing the job, he asked the Amalekite soldier to slay him which the soldier did (2 Samuel 1:10).

I have often seen something similar happen when someone goes to a fortune-teller for a reading. As time passes, the receiver of the message will often unconsciously manipulate events in his or her life in order to make the predictions come true.

In my lectures, there are those who have conjectured that the woman from Endor was demonically possessed. This is, of course, possible, but it must be pointed out that neither Satan nor his demons can predict future events. (In the section of the book dealing with the powers of demons, this point will be pursued further.) There is only one other possibility, and that is that the woman was speaking in a trancelike state, and that she was not aware of what she was saying. This last viewpoint is inconsistent, however, with the rest of the Scripture, because as we have mentioned earlier, whenever the term, "ones that have a familiar spirit," is used, it is always used with recognized frauds, i.e. wizards.

There is even stronger evidence that makes for a tighter case concerning the contacting of spirits, as far as the Christian position is concerned. Jesus, during His ministry, taught through the use of parables. In doing so, He utilized a technique which I like to call *three-quarter teaching*. He told His hearers three-quarters of a story, and then He let them work out the last quarter for themselves so that the lesson became theirs. Whenever He made specific reference to someone's name, the account was regarded as a true story rather than a fictitious parable. Such a true account can be found in Luke 16:19–31.

> There was a certain rich man, which was clothed in purple and fine linen, and fared sumptuously every day: And there was a certain beggar named Lazarus, which was laid at his gate, full of sores, And desiring to be fed with the crumbs which fell from the rich man's table: moreover the dogs came and licked his sores. And it came to pass, that the beggar died, and was carried by the angels into Abraham's bosom: the rich man also died, and was buried; And in hell he lift up his eyes, being in torments, and seeth Abraham afar off, and Lazarus in his bosom. And he cried and said, Father Abraham, have mercy on me, and send Lazarus, that he may dip the tip of his finger in water,

and cool my tongue; for I am tormented in this flame. But Abraham said, Son, remember that thou in thy lifetime receivedst thy good things, and likewise Lazarus evil things: but now he is comforted, and thou art tormented. And beside all this, between us and you there is a great gulf fixed: so that they which would pass from hence to you cannot; neither can they pass to us, that would come from thence. Then he said, I pray thee therefore, father, that thou wouldest send him to my father's house: For I have five brethren; that he may testify unto them, lest they also come into this place of torment. Abraham saith unto him, They have Moses and the prophets; let them hear them. And he said, Nay, father Abraham: but if one went unto them from the dead, they will repent. And he said unto him, If they hear not Moses and the prophets, neither will they be persuaded, though one rose from the dead.

In this account, the rich man had two requests that were denied. He first asked if Lazarus would "cool my tongue" and this was denied because of the "great gulf" between heaven and hell. From the original Greek, *gulf* may also be translated "impassable interval." The rich man then made another request. He asked Abraham to send Lazarus back to his family and warn them so they may repent and not be sent to hell. This last request was also denied. There is no passage of Scripture where one is able physically to converse with the spirit of someone who is deceased. Jesus did, however, command His friend Lazarus (not the same Lazarus as in the above account) who had died and was buried in a tomb for four days to come back to life (John 11:38-44). Because of His power, Jesus raised Lazarus from the dead. And because He is God incarnate, it is my opinion that He also has the power to converse with a spirit. But please note that He did not choose to do so. There would be no purpose in it.

In Deuteronomy 18:11, 12 the Lord condemns wizards and those "with familiar spirits," not because of some supernatural power they possess, but because they perform what the Lord considers abominations. In other words, that which is idolatrous and paganistic and not that which will glorify the living God.

My findings, both through research and searching Scripture, have yielded the same results as others, including Houdini, who have experienced the ins and outs of deception. Few people are aware of the fact that Houdini, through many self-proclaimed mediums, had tried to contact his deceased mother. His experiences with these unscrupulous characters led to his fervent exposure of all the famous frauds of the day.

Dr. Koch's work in this area is totally invalid. He is not qualified to speak about contacting spirits of the dead. As a Christian, he does not have a biblical example to stand upon. Harm was inflicted upon his patients because the victims sought a source of power outside of the Lord, which in and of itself brings spiritual separation. This, in turn, can give rise to psychiatric problems, particularly when an individual believes he is receiving powers or intimate knowledge from an outside, supernatural force, regardless of whether the power is fictitious or not. I do believe that contact can be made with satanic forces and this will be dealt with later. But contact with spirits of the dead has never been authenticated and contradicts the testimony of Scripture. Because of this fact, mediums contacting the dead via table tilting, Ouija boards or séances are as valid as haunted houses.

Milbourne Christopher's friend, Hulbert Footner, was described by him as "an author who lived in an eighteenth-century house in southern Maryland .... where a friendly ghost was company during long nights when he was working on a novel." Milbourne asked him, "What would you do if the spirit turned hostile, set fire to your books, kept you awake with its banging, and tossed lamps around your den?"

"Make note immediately," he answered with a smile. "There's a great audience for accounts of unexplained phenomena."[25]

Danny Korem

PSYCHIATRIC COMMENT

The death of a loved one is one of the most traumatic emotional experiences of life. In almost every such occurrence, the intimate survivor is left with temporary feelings of moderate to severe denial, anger (including anger toward God), guilt, and grief (sorrow).

Overwhelmed by these various stages of the grief reaction, a sane person who would normally not be so gullible can often be quite vulnerable to the deceit of mediums and other frauds. Many sociopathic embezzlers make their "friendly" moves during a grief reaction in a vulnerable person's life. Even college students, when suffering a severe loss (such as the breaking of an engagement) are vulnerable to ridiculous cults like the Moonies or Hare Krishna.

One patient whom I treated was a young girl whose father died of a heart attack when she was five years old. His dying words to his daughter as the ambulance carried him off were, "Don't worry, dear; I'll be back." She refused to accept his death when told of it, and developed auditory and visual hallucinations of her father coming into her bedroom to tuck her in each night and comfort her. She honestly believed it was he. With intensive therapy and major tranquilizers, she finally ceased having these hallucinations.

About 3 percent of the American population is psychotic or borderline psychotic at any one time. Many of these persons really believe they communicate with the dead, "hearing" the voices of deceased loved ones as clearly as if they were audible. These are known as *auditory hallucinations*. For some strange reason, these voices nearly always disappear when the psychotic person takes antipsychotic medications for a few days. Deceased "spirits" must really hate that stuff!

Out of all the hundreds of psychiatric patients I have talked to who believed they had communicated with deceased loved ones (with or without the "assistance" of a medium), not a single case ended up being even halfway believable—especially when the communications with the dead spirits cease after a few days on antipsychotic medications.

Paul Meier, M.D.

11
Look Into My Eyes As I Look Into Your Pocketbook

Have you ever wondered why people are so willing to believe purported prophetic statements concerning the future? The answer lies in man's uncertainty of what the future may bring and man's search for a sense of security and power through its knowledge. There is no one who can predict with absolute reliability what anyone's future will bring.

The fourth chapter of the Book of James warns against such activity.

> Now listen, you who say, "Today or tomorrow we will go to this or that city, spend a year there, carry on business and make money." Why, you do not even know what will happen tomorrow. What is your life? You are a mist that appears for a little while and then vanishes. Instead, you ought to say, "If it is the Lord's will, we will live and do this or that."
>
> James 4:13—15 NIV

Several years ago I received a call to appear before the woman's auxiliary of a powerboat association. I agreed to go and do some card and coin tricks. During the course of the performance, one of the gals commented that she had heard me on a talk show airing my views concerning the fraud in so-called psychic pursuits. She asked me if it was possible to "read the cards." She was referring to tarot cards used by fortune-tellers. I tried explaining to her that it is impossible to foretell the future with such cards, but she persisted. I then proceeded to give a demonstration to make my point.

Tarot cards are used by some in attempts to foretell the future. Here are a few of the seventy-eight different cards, laid out as during a demonstration of "reading the cards."

I asked for the lady's tarot cards. I then shuffled them as all of the women present pressed closer to watch. One at a time, I began turning the cards over in what appeared to be a careful pattern. Actually, I was merely laying them out in a way which might trigger something of significance for someone present.

I stated, "I see in the cards that someone has a neighbor who is ill." There was a short, audible gasp from one of the onlookers.

Proceeding ahead in an obviously mysterious manner, I continued: "Yes, It appears that this person is in the hospital and has a very short time to live. Does this apply to anybody here?"

"That's me," replied an older lady about sixty years of age. To look at her and the intrigue building in her facial expression, it was easy to imagine that she belonged to the soap-opera set and unnecessarily involved herself in the lives of others.

"It appears that this friend has an ailment of the heart," I continued. Noticing that there was little facial change in her expression or breathing, I shifted gears and said, "No, it appears that it is a cancerous tumor."

"That's right! That is what she has," she responded as if dazed.

"Yes, it is a female who has the ailment, and I detect that the cancer is in the bone," I continued somewhat morbidly. It was obvious that the poor lady was on the verge of becoming emotionally overwhelmed, so I refused to press forward any more.

The ladies were very persistent about my doing another reading, so I did two more concerning less important events. I accurately told one gal that she and her husband were in the process of purchasing a new car and they could not decide between two specific models. I even named the cars in question. For another, I related the difficulty she was having in deciding how she was going to redecorate her kitchen. When I finished, all were completely amazed at how the cards could unravel such mysteries. I then proceeded to explain how I was able to disclose information relating to people and events without any prior knowledge of them. I explained what is known in my profession as cold reading.

The art of cold reading is the ability to extract information from someone without his or her being aware of the process. In the chapter on muscle reading we covered how the entertainer recognizes certain reactions of the participant which, through experience, enable him to locate hidden objects. Paul Meier mentioned in chapter 2 that there are many sensory clues that a trained psychiatrist will identify and use to provide for him bits of information concerning his patient. It is an application of these same principles which enables the fortune-teller to divulge information to the subject that seemingly is impossible to perceive.

In this demonstration, notice the position in which a fortune-teller had held Danny Korem's hand during reading. The position enabled her to sense any flinching or movement in the hand—a technique similar to that used in muscle reading.

To illustrate, I will break down the reading I presented to the ladies. Please understand that I do *not* recommend anyone doing this "just for fun" or to see what will happen. If this sort of thing is done, and it involves a person who has psychological problems, serious and damnable consequences could result. The reason for my detailing this area of pseudo-occult practices is to destroy the belief that an individual might possess supernatural power which enables him to perceive hidden thoughts or forecast future events.

The first reading, concerning the neighbor with cancer, was much easier to extract that one might suspect. The ladies in the auxiliary were of an average age of forty years. It is a matter of statistics that the mortality rate increases with age. This is a fact of life. The odds were great that there would be someone present who would have a friend who was seriously ill, even in critical condition. So I decided to pursue this line of patter.

The tarot cards consist of seventy-eight cards, each symbolizing something different—death, wealth, anger, and so forth. As can be seen in the photographs, they are somewhat bizarre in appearance. I have no knowledge of the precise meaning of the cards in a deck, and neither do I care. They merely help further superstitious thought, and there are more pressing matters on which I would rather expend my energies. What is important to understand is that many of the women gathered at this show really believed that the cards could tell them something. As I turned over the cards, I improvised and tailored my patter to reflect the sensory and psychological clues coming from those gathered.

After I had randomly displayed some cards, I tried to piece together a story line around the potential death of someone who was ill. When I mentioned that one of those present had a neighbor stricken with an incurable disease and one of the women audibly gasped, I knew my job would be an easy one. As I let the imagined story unfold (I say *imagined* because it was just that), her breathing quickened slightly, which is a sure sign that I was on the right track. With some people you can tell if you are "on" when you see their eyelids raise slightly, or if their face remains absolutely passive. I then made a sound guess when I said that her friend appeared to be in the hospital and that she was greatly concerned about her. As you can see in the photo depicting the layout of the cards, there is a card that shows a woman fretting, another of a girl crying and one of death. These cards could represent almost anything because they are vague, and they served to fit my story line. I used the card with the two ladies talking to illustrate that a neighbor had told her of the illness. Again any statement of that kind would fit. I used the card that shows the broken chair and an angry woman to state that the woman afflicted would not give up and the victory card to state that it might be possible for her to recover with perseverance.

I was able to correctly guess the ailment because of the woman's reaction to my statements. When I mentioned that it appeared that the one afflicted had heart problems, probably due to a fierce temper (referring to the card where the woman appears angry with the broken chair), the gal's eyelids slightly narrowed telling me that I was off the track, so I threw out another guess that it might be cancer. To this, her reaction was positive. Please note that when I missed, I continued on as if I was not even aware of her presence or my inaccurate statement. I said, "No, this card is trying to tell us of her willingness to fight back."

The cards also act as another sounding board as far as the reader is concerned. The reader is not only able to play off of what is being said, but also off of the reactions of the subject as the cards are displayed. The cards also provide a way out if the reader is incorrect in his line of patter by enabling him to backtrack and explain what the cards meant to tell him. The reader simply admits that he was not perceptive enough to receive this information. What all this boils down to is a glorified con game, where those gullible enough to believe are duped. The other purported readings at this particular gathering were carried out in the same manner.

When I was through, I explained these step-by-step procedures to the ladies so there would be no misunderstanding about my having any powers. What follows is a simplified list of the techniques generally used by fortune-tellers who give readings:

1. Observation of sensory clues.
2. Prior knowledge of subject obtained secretly before reading.
3. Ability to think on one's feet and chance direction of the reading without hesitation or detection.
4. Understanding of human nature.
5. Utilization of the cards or any other apparatus to pick up sensory clues or change the direction of the reading when off the track.
6. An element of luck and a keen sense of playing the odds so that a well-placed guess may produce spectacular results.

There are many readers of tea leaves, cards, and crystal balls, who genuinely believe that they can execute a reading without assistance from their peculiar little trinkets. They really believe that they have a power, unaware that they are utilizing principles of cold reading which are common knowledge to many magicians.

To illustrate this point, I looked in our newspaper's television viewing guide and after reading through the advertisements, selected the name of one of the purported seers and made an appointment with a Sister Ruth. Before I went to see her, I made a list of the points on which I would subliminally try to cue her. The fictitious scenario was as follows:

1. I was deeply troubled and worried.
2. I had just lost a job.
3. My occupation was selling cleaning supplies to small businesses.
4. A man would call me in the near future with a good job offer.
5. The offer would come from a similar field but not in the same line of work.
6. I must be considerate of my family (wife, two boys, and one daughter) during this time.
7. My wife is blonde with short hair.

Points 3 and 7 were added to determine her level of expertise at picking up my sensory clues. I dressed casually, choosing moderately sharp-looking clothing that showed some wear, the type that one might associate with a not-too-successful salesman. I borrowed a neighbor's eight-year-old car to make it appear that I didn't have much money.

Sister Ruth lived in a house in a run-down part of town. It had a "for sale" sign in front. When I rang the door bell, a woman of about thirty-five years of age, with a weather-beaten face and of medium stature, invited me in. Except for a couch, there was no furniture in the living room into which I was escorted. Two children, about eight and ten years of age, whom I presumed to be hers, were told to play outside. Sister Ruth asked me to sit on the couch and then sat down about a foot and a half from me. I was careful to make sure that I had a clear path to the door in case I was propositioned!

The first thing she asked of me was to "take out a ten-dollar-bill and make a wish right here." As she said this, she took my hand and held it palm up between her hands as shown in the photograph. I took a ten from my wallet and placed it on my hand. Proceeding, I closed my eyes and pretended to make a wish. Notice that her hands were in a position that would enable her to sense any flinching or movement in my hand, a technique similar to that used by the muscle reader. I thought that this was a very clever application of this technique, because she not only was able to hold my hand, but she offered a logical reason for my taking out the bill and placing it on my hand—to make a wish, of course!

She then started with her spiel, telling me things that could apply and appeal to anybody: I was kind, thoughtful, possibly overaggressive, and so forth. Then she told me that I was troubled. Bingo! She got point number one. Why else does someone go to these "bucksters" (I use this word because that is what they extract from you) except out of curiosity? It was unlikely, though, that a man would come in the middle of the day, driven just by curiosity. The most probable reason was that I had a marital problem.

She tried hammering in on the possibility that I was having some kind of problem with my wife. I let my eyes widen at this point. She thought that she was on the track. She pursued this area until she realized that I was not responding. She then said "No, the problem is not just with your wife, but there is something else. Your job. Something is wrong where you work." At this point I made a slight twitch in my hand. She picked this up and carried the ball by saying, "You lost your job because of your boss. Yes, that's it." Point two was perceived. Unfortunately, she was not a very good reader because she never got points three or four even though I did my best to let her pick them up. It was somewhere between point one and two that she took my ten dollars and continued with the reading. She was very shrewd in her handling of this most important point. Only after she thought she had me convinced that she could help me with my problem, did she take the money. Over the next four or five minutes she hit points five and six but completely missed point seven. The entire session lasted only twelve minutes. She is the only reader whom I have ever visited outside of a newspaper interview I did in

New Orleans. The only reason I went was to verify the fact that one could be cued either knowingly or unknowingly and present a purported psychic reading. I *do not* recommend anyone going to these individuals for any reason, because serious harm may—intentionally or unintentionally—come about.

Those who claim to be able to foresee the future are not only found in dimly lit tearooms and old, secluded houses, but they can also be found blatantly selling their wares in the homes of the rich (sometimes the easiest and most unsuspecting prey) as well as in our newspapers and magazines. There is a very famous health spa noted for catering to the woman of means and influence at which I entertain and speak on occasion. Whenever the discussion comes to the supernatural, many of these dignified and affluent ladies will tell a story of some psychic adventure they had witnessed. Several of these ladies even admit to having invited some of these spurious characters to their homes. One name that always seems to come up when discussing prognosticators is Jeane Dixon.

Much recognition has been given Jeane Dixon concerning her purported ability to prognosticate the future. Ruth Montgomery, in the foreword of her book *The Gift of Prophecy* identifies her subject as a "modern-day psychic whose visions apparently lift the curtain of tomorrow ..."[26]

In the paperback edition which was very popular in the 60s there are teaser sheets on which many of Mrs. Dixon's predictions are reprinted. The first page reads as follows:

IF YOU DON'T BELIEVE THAT ANYONE CAN PREDICT THE FUTURE WITH A CRYSTAL BALL ... THEN READ THESE STARTLING, OFTEN FRIGHTENING, PRECOGNITIONS OF EVENTS BY THE PHENOMENAL—

JEANE DIXON

— The assassination of President Kennedy ...

— Nehru's death and his succession by Shastri

— That China would go communistic

— The assassination of Mahatma Ghandi

— Russia's launching the world's first satellite

— Eisenhower's election; his heart attack, and his recovery

— The Kremlin shake-up ending with Khrushchev's dismissal and Suslov's takeover[27]

What is not stated here is how many other predictions Mrs. Dixon may have made over this period of time, and the accuracy of them. We are not given her track record. The proof that she does not have the ability to predict the future with any more reliability than anyone reading this text can be found on the second teaser page of this same edition. Here she goes on record with her other predictions of the future.

THE AMAZING JEANE DIXON PREDICTS THE FUTURE

— Russia will be the first nation to put men on the moon.

— 1967 will be a year of grave national peril for America ... perhaps the decisive year.

— The Berlin Wall will come down.

— The Republican Party will win at the polls in 1968.

— The test-ban treaty will prove bad for America and will be used against us.

— Red China will invade Russian territory.

— Red China will wage "germ warfare."

— Russia will become our ally.

— Pope Paul, President Johnson and Sargent Shriver are now in great personal danger.

— A child born in the Middle East of humble peasant stock on February 5, 1962 will revolutionize the world.[28]

Let us examine these predictions of Mrs. Dixon. Owing to the vagueness of them, they could be interpreted in a number of different ways.

The first prediction needs no clarification. It was just an outright miss.

The second prediction concerning the peril of the United States could be interpreted to mean that the Seven Day War in Israel was the great danger because it was also a global danger. But Mrs. Dixon claims that her gift is from God. Wouldn't He have made it clear that it was Israel that was in danger and not the United States? Mrs. Dixon could probably appease her followers by saying later that the country she thought she saw in her crystal ball was the United States but that it must have been Israel.

Prediction number three has so far been shown to be inaccurate, although we must remember that there is no time limit on when the wall will come down. If thirty years down the road, the wall is taken down, Mrs. Dixon's followers can further extol her gift.

Prediction number four is just as vague. It states, "The Republican party will win at the polls in 1968." Presidentially, they did, but not in the House or the Senate. If she was referring to the presidential election, why didn't she say so? Because there is safety in being vague.

The test-ban-treaty prediction again is very vague and could be argued from both sides of the fence.

The prediction that Red China will invade Russia again has no time or date limitation put on it. Common sense dictates that China will never invade Russia as long as Russia maintains superior nuclear strength. It would be suicidal.

The prediction that Russia will become our ally is grossly inaccurate, especially in light of the recent invasion of Afghanistan by Russia and the clear move by that country to dominate the oil-rich Middle East. But again she places no time limit on her prophecy.

The one prediction that may come to pass is her prediction concerning China waging germ warfare, but in fifteen years since the public announcement of her prediction, this has yet to happen.

It is amusing that she stated that President Johnson, Pope Paul and Sargent Shriver were in "great personal danger." In 1965 when this prediction was published, all three men were in the public eye. Every president is in great personal danger every day, which is the reason we spend millions of dollars every year for his protection by the Secret Service. This danger factor unfortunately applies to many other public figures who receive a great deal of exposure in the media. Using the name of a current public figure in a prediction will cause a great deal of comment. Of the hundreds of predictions Mrs. Dixon has made, one remarkable prediction that she is credited with appeared in the May 13, 1956 issue of *Parade* magazine.

> As to the 1960 election, Mrs. Dixon thinks it will be dominated by labor and won by a Democrat. But he will be assassinated or die in office, though not necessarily in his first term.

Before one gets all excited and exclaims, "How does she do it," let us listen to what Milbourne Christopher has to say about her in his book, *ESP, Seers and Psychics.*

As we know now, the election was not "dominated by labor." She did not name the Democrat she said would win; no date was given for the president-to-be's end; and his announced demise was qualified with Delphic ingenuity "assassinated or die in office, though not necessarily in his first term." Thus if the president served a single term, it would be within four years; if he was re-elected, there was an eight year span.

Such a surmise was not illogical for anyone who has studied recent American history. William McKinley was assassinated a year after the turn of the century. Warren Gamaliel Harding and Franklin Delano Roosevelt died in office, and during Harry S. Truman's tenure an attempt was made on his life. Moreover, the normal burdens of the presidency are such that it is commonly regarded as a man-killing office. Woodrow Wilson and Dwight Eisenhower were critically ill during their terms. Unfortunately for the nation, the odds against Mrs. Dixon's prophecy's being fulfilled were not too great—7-3 based on twentieth-century experience.[29]

Added to the above facts, there was an assassination attempt on President Ford's life. Mr. Christopher later continues:

> In January 1960 Mrs. Dixon changed her mind. Kennedy, then a contender for the Democrat nomination, would not be elected in November, she said in Ruth Montgomery's syndicated column. In June she stated that "The symbol of the presidency is directly over the head of Vice-President Nixon" but "unless the Republican party really gets out and puts forth every effort it will topple." Fire enough shots, riflemen agree, and eventually you will hit the bull's-eye.[30]

Hopefully, this will lay to rest the concern over Mrs. Dixon's ability to accurately predict future events.

Her last prediction—relating to the birth of a peasant in the Middle East—again is a safe bet to make. She won't live—if she lives a normal life span—to see if that prediction comes true or not, but it will cause a lot of foolish people to speculate.

What is particularly distressing to me is that Mrs. Dixon claims that this gift comes from God, the Creator of the universe. The Apostle Peter warns against false prophets:

> But there were false prophets also among the people, even as there shall be false teachers among you, who privily shall bring in damnable heresies, even denying the Lord that brought them, and bring upon themselves swift destruction. And many shall follow their pernicious ways; by reason of whom the way of truth shall be evil spoken of. And through covetousness they shall with feigned words make merchandise of you ....
>
>   2 Peter 2:1-3

When discussing the area of fortune-telling in a lecture format, someone invariably will make a statement like the following: "I see how most cases of fortune-telling can be explained by cold reading, but I had this woman who had never seen me before—" whereupon, this person will launch into a description of some reading that was stunningly accurate. Or one person might tell of some thought expressed by the fortune-teller—the death of a relative—and the relative had indeed just passed away. I am then asked to explain.

Experience will teach anyone who investigates these types of stories that even the most credible persons are prone to exaggerate the actual events or thoughts they had with the passing of time. This makes it exceedingly difficult to document these cases. There is also the matter of probability. There are three points I would like to make in this area of purported prognostications or clairvoyance.

First, each of us has millions of experiences and thoughts in our lifetime. Probability alone will suggest that eventually a thought and an event will coincide. When this happens, many believe that this is a result of some deeply secluded power which can be brought to the surface and cultivated. The real answer is, of course, the law of probability. There is not a mother or father who, at one time or another, has not had a premonition of his or her child being harmed only to have this thought laid to rest when the child returns home from school or a friend's house safely and without incident. Rarely, if ever, does a random thought about some imagined event and the materialization of that event actually occur. When it does happen, most people acknowledge it for what it is—a product of chance.

My second point is this. In a given population there will be those whose "hit" ratio (a thought and an event matching up) will be higher than others simply because of the law of probability. This is true in any game of chance. When a clever fortune-teller combines good cold-reading techniques with a chance guess or two, he or she will appear to almost unerringly pick up someone's thoughts and prognosticate the future, but there will be other times when he or she will fail. My question is this: If such powers exist, why are they so fleeting, and why can't they be tested? The reason is a simple one. They don't exist. In the twelve years I have devoted to researching this subject, I have neither seen a valid case of prognostication, nor have I been confronted with hard-core documentation to substantiate a purported case. The predicting of a future event is possible, but only within a limited context which will be discussed in the chapter, "The Future Spoken."

As I will demonstrate in the next section of text, for one to have the gift of prophecy according to the Scriptures, the predictions of this individual must *infallibly* come to pass. There cannot be a *percentage* of accuracy. Common sense dictates that if the Sovereign Lord of the universe wished to impart future knowledge, He could do it perfectly every time, without failure, even allowing for our imperfect state. In His perfect wisdom, He could select those who would accurately relay His message to us. Biblical prophecy is not only stunning; it has been 100 percent accurate. No other document in the history of mankind can make this claim.

I realize that, up to this point, the reader may have reached the conclusion that I disregard the possibility of a manifestation of a supernatural nature. This is not the case. I do believe that the *majority* of those stories reporting supernatural phenomena can be explained. However, there is a strong case for the supernatural, that can be stated through: (1) philosophic reasoning—which necessitates a step of faith no matter how convincing the philosophic argument; (2) through physical facts that point to the reality of the supernatural. Please bear in mind that the conclusions I have reached are not mere conjecture based upon blind faith, but they are supported with hard evidence plus a background of understanding how the mind can be deceived.

Danny Korem

PSYCHIATRIC COMMENT

Out of the four billion persons on planet earth, there are four billion who have inferiority feelings. Nearly all humans (except those with massive denial systems) will readily admit that they feel inferior and insecure some of the time. It is all a matter of degree. The more inferior a person feels intrapsychically, the more of a tendency he will have to search for supernatural phenomena in his coincidental everyday experiences. We often joke about the extreme Calvinist who trips on his shoelaces, falls down a flight of stairs, gets back up, brushes himself off, and says to himself, "Thank God that is over with!" He interprets even his own clumsy tripping on his shoelaces as a direct act of God because it compensates for his inferiority feelings and makes him feel more significant. We Christians tend to blame

God or the devil for many of our mistakes. As Flip Wilson, the comedian, frequently jokes, "The devil made me do it." Does this mean that every event in our lives is coincidental? No, of course not! We would be equally naive to go to the opposite extreme and assume that God *never* brings persons or events into our lives to mature us. David states in Psalms 139:17, 18 that God thinks about us so many times each day that we cannot even count them!

As a psychiatrist, I have found non-Christians to be just as "superspiritual" as some of the Christians I have known, but in their own way. Even educated people with more severe inferiority feelings will interpret coincidental events in their lives as though they had a "sixth sense" or ESP. Some of them even consult with purported mediums, tarot cards, astrological charts in the daily newspaper, or other absurd sources to make major life decisions. Believing in these purported extrasensory phenomena, and believing that they somehow relate to the individual personally, brings a temporary sense of significance to an insecure individual, highly educated or not. I am sure the Ayatollah Khomeini was very well educated, and yet look at the absurdly paranoid exaggerations he has of the realities around him.

Approximately 3 percent of the world population will actually have a "psychotic break" of some sort during their lifetimes. By *psychotic break* I am referring to an actual break with reality. Many of these psychoses come about when an individual feels so extremely insignificant and self-deprecatory in his real-world experiences that he "breaks" with reality and believes he will be the next president, or that he is Christ, or that the TV news commentators are talking about him symbolically through certain words or phrases, or that the FBI is bugging his phone. He believes these things to feel significant and to kill the severe emotional pain that inferiority feelings bring. In psychiatric terminology, he has "ideas of reference," a common symptom of schizophrenia, thinking to a delusional proportion that nearly all of the coincidental life-events occurring around somehow are occurring because of him.

One such patient, for example, escaped from a state hospital, drove a car the wrong way down a one-way highway, and thought all the people driving the opposite (and correct) way were trying to stop her. She rammed her car purposely into the oncoming traffic, killing an innocent driver in another car. She was having "ideas of reference," and they resulted in accidental murder.

Danny Korem's description of the ability of trained fortune-tellers to do cold reading is exactly correct. Even though each person is in some ways unique, humans tend to fall into very common, typical mannerisms and behavior patterns. After I treated my first hundred patients for a year or so each, I discovered that I had already seen nearly every human pattern there was to be seen. In the years that have followed, I have yet to see or hear anything new. People of various personality types have predictable behavior patterns, predictable family backgrounds, predictable thought processes, predictable ways of handling emotions, and even predictable body language. As a psychiatrist, I can "cold read" a new patient by getting him to discuss various areas of conflict. When he gets on a subject his unconscious is defending himself against, his pupils will dilate, his neck may blotch somewhat, his hands may become more tense, he may develop slight tears in his eyes, and he will rapidly change the subject. I use these clues to home in on that conflict, giving the patient permission to go ahead and cry if that subject makes him feel sad, and encouraging verbalization so he can resolve the unconscious conflict to a point where it doesn't hurt to discuss that conflict area any more. A common, unconscious conflict, for example, is repressed anger toward a controlling parent. The individual with this conflict would fear becoming aware of this repressed anger toward a parent (to cover up his true resentment). To become aware of his true repressed anger would cause unconscious fear of rejection by that parent, which would— temporarily—be emotionally painful because so much of a person's self-concept is based (erroneously) on what his parents thought of him in his formative years.

For some examples of predictable behavior traits in two common personality types, here are two partial lists, one relating to the hysterical (dramatic) female, and the other to the obsessive-compulsive (workaholic) male.

The hysterical female:

1. The hysterical individual is likeable.
2. She has a good personality.
3. She is outgoing.
4. She is the life of the party.
5. She is fun to be with.
6. The hysterical personality is dramatic.
7. She is theatrical.
8 She is sanguine.
9. She is unstable.
10. She is emotional.
11. She is excitable.
12. She emphasizes the present.
13. She emphasizes *feelings*.
14. She is vain.
15. She is self-centered.
16. She is dependent.
17. She is naive.
18. She is manipulative.
19. She may overdose as a suicide gesture.
20. The hysterical individual is seductive in dress.

The obsessive-compulsive male:

1. He is perfectionistic.
2. He is neat.
3. He is clean.
4. He is orderly.
5. He is dutiful.
6. He is conscientious.
7. He is meticulous.
8. The obsessive-compulsive individual does a good job.
9. But he works too hard.
10. And is unable to relax .

11. He is choleric.
12. He is overly conscientious.
13. He is overly concerned.
14. His conscience is overly strict.
15. His thinking is rigid.
16. He is inflexible.
17. He frequently rationalizes to deceive himself and defend himself.
18. He intellectualizes to avoid emotions.
19. The obsessive-compulsive is a good student.
20. He is well organized.[31]

No individual would possess *all* of the *obsessive-compulsive or all* of the *hysterical* traits. However, if a reader noticed a number of these traits in a person he or she had just met, the medium could do a cold reading and guess with good probability that many of the other traits that fit that personality would also be present. The reader's natural insights into human nature astonish the naive visitor, just as my patients frequently ask me if I can somehow read their minds.

Paul Meier, M.D.

12
The Future Spoken—Compelling Evidence

In his thought-provoking book *Broca's Brain*, Dr. Carl Sagan, one of the world's leading astronomers, who played a key role in the Mariner, Viking, and Voyager expeditions, states that he is not familiar with any "compelling evidence for anthropomorphic patriarchs controlling human destiny from some hidden celestial vantage point. ..."[32] He later states that, "Religion has been scarred in its confrontation with science, and many people—but by no means all—are reluctant to accept a body of theological belief that is too obviously in conflict with what else we know."[33]

Further in his text he asks, "Why is the opposition to rational discourse and reasoned argument in religion so strong?"[34] He contends that "religions ought to be subject to at least the same degree of skepticism as, for example, contentions about UFO visitations. ..."[35]

Many who believe the Bible to be true and accurate and the inspired Word of God might react vehemently to these statements. What one must understand is that there is much solid knowledge to support the biblicist's view, that is not widely known, regardless of one's intellectual capacity or education.

From Dr. Sagan's perspective it is probably a true statement that he has never been confronted with "compelling evidence." This may be due in part to personal prejudice or more simply because he has never heard the facts. As will be demonstrated in this chapter, biblical prophecy, at least, has not "been scarred" by science. To the contrary, the science of archaeology has actually helped to confirm the predictions that will be analyzed. It may be true that religion—a vast and nebulous term—may be discredited by the finds of science, but not the truth or the historical facts communicated in the Bible.

The reason many people of a religious nature may disdain "rational discourse" and "reasoned argument" is that they either don't have the facts to back up their claims to a particular religious belief, or they are just ignorant of the facts and become frustrated when trying to prove that what they "know" is true. The latter applies to Christians at large. It is important to take note that by *Christians* we are not referring to that mass conglomeration of religions that espouse Christian beliefs but rather those individuals who believe that Christ lived and died and rose from the grave on the third day, and that one must accept Christ as Savior in order to have eternal life with God after death. The Bible only uses the term *Christian* three times in the entire New Testament text. It is the Christian, as just defined, who particularly sets up barriers to skepticism and argument owing to the fact that most do not know the facts that substantiate the claims to their faith or how to effectively reason with someone who initially approaches the claims of the Scriptures from a cerebral point of view. For one of a non-Christian background, the Bible can appear to be a maze with no more authority than any of the other thousands of "religious" books man has followed.

The goal of this chapter is to give thinking persons compelling evidence that will cause the Bible to be looked upon in a new light. I was fortunate in harnessing the time, resources, and assistance of Josh McDowell, one of the world's leading apologetic authorities. Apologetics is the study of the historic authenticity of the Christian faith from a factual perspective. McDowell's texts were developed out of an unusual course of events. As a brilliant university student, he set out to disprove the Christian faith with arguments based upon historical facts. After two years he found the physical evidence so overwhelming, that he became a Christian as earlier defined. Now, many years later, McDowell is acknowledged to be one of the foremost university campus lecturers speaking before an estimated three-quarters of a million people every year. It is upon McDowell's and Mark Lundeen's research that we will base this section of the text.

The area of discussion we will pursue in this chapter is biblical prophecy. The reason this particular subject has been chosen is because one can analyze specific facts of a historical nature and then make an intelligent decision based upon these facts rather than one's own philosophy. A random statement such as, "I would believe in biblical prophecy if it could be proven scientifically," does not apply.

> Scientific proof is based on showing that something is a fact by repeating the event in the presence of the person questioning the fact. There is a controlled environment where observations can be made, data drawn, and hypotheses empirically verified.[36]

> The scientific method, however it is defined, is related to measurement of phenomena and experimentation or repeated observation.[37]

When dealing with a historical event and a prediction made before the event in question, one must apply legal-historical proof, a term coined by McDowell.

> Testing the truth of a hypothesis by the use of controlled experiments is one of the key techniques of the modern scientific method. For example, somebody says, "Ivory soap doesn't float." So I take the person to the kitchen, put eight inches of water in the sink at 82.7°, and drop in the soap. Plunk. Observations are made, data are drawn, and a hypothesis is empirically verified: Ivory soap floats.

> Now if the scientific method was the only method of proving something, you couldn't prove that you went to your first hour class this morning or that you had lunch today. There's no way you can repeat those events in a controlled situation.

> Now here's what is called the legal-historical proof, which is based on showing that something is fact beyond a reasonable doubt. In other words, a verdict is reached on the basis of the weight of the evidence. That is, there's no reasonable basis for doubting the decision. It depends upon three types of testimony: oral testimony, written testimony, and exhibits (such as a gun, bullet, notebook). Using the legal method of determining what happened, you could pretty well

prove beyond a reasonable doubt that you were in class this morning: your friends saw you, you have your notes, the professor remembers you.

The scientific method can be used only to prove repeatable things; it isn't adequate for proving or disproving many questions about a person or event in history. The scientific method isn't appropriate for answering such questions as "Did George Washington live?" "Was Martin Luther King a civil rights leader?" "Who was Jesus of Nazareth?" "Was Robert Kennedy attorney general of the U.S.A.?" "Was Jesus Christ raised from the dead?" These are out of the realm of scientific proof, and we need to put them in the realm of legal proof.[38]

As we will be dealing with predictions of specific historical events, we shall define history as, "knowledge of the past based upon testimony." As McDowell stated, there are three kinds of testimony. We shall only be concerned with the qualifications of written testimony, since we will deal with predictions that were written. There are three tests to establish the validity of written testimony. They are the bibliographical test, internal-evidence test, and external test. The bibliographical test can be defined as follows:

> The bibliographical test is an examination of the textual transmission by which documents reach us. In other words, not having the original documents, how reliable are the copies we have in regard to the number of manuscripts (MSS) and the time interval between the original and extant (existing) copy?[39]

As an English major in college, I was taught that Homer had written the *Iliad*. This is based upon the fact that we have 643 manuscripts which are ascribed to Homer, the earliest of which dates to 400 B.C.. As the *Iliad* was originally penned by Homer around 900 B.C., a gap of 500 years exists between the original text and the extant (existing) text. The New Testament, in comparison, offers us over 24,000 manuscripts. William Albright, one of the world's foremost biblical archaeologists, stated:

> We can already say emphatically that there is no longer any solid basis for dating any book of the New Testament after about A.D. 80.[40]

Sir Frederic Kenyon, who was the director and principal librarian at the British Museum and second to none in authority in issuing statements about manuscripts, concludes:

> The interval then between dates or original composition and the earliest extant evidence becomes so small as to be in fact negligible, and the last foundation for any doubt that the Scriptures have come down to us substantially as they were written has now been removed. Both the authenticity and the general integrity of the Books of the New Testament may be regarded as finally established.[41]

We shall deal with the bibliographical test for the New Testament a little later.

The *internal-evidence test* determines whether the written record is credible and to what extent. John W. Montgomery states:

> One must listen to the claims of the document under analysis, and not assume fraud or error unless the author disqualified himself by contradictions or known factual inaccuracies.[42]

The internal evidence test will be applied to both the Old and New Testament to verify the historical content and accuracy of transmission of both texts.

The last test is that of external evidence. Here we are concerned with "whether other historical material confirms or denies the internal testimony of the documents themselves. In other words, what sources are there, apart from the literature under analysis, that substantiate its accuracy, reliability, and authenticity."[43]

We will apply each test to both the Old and New Testament. As you follow carefully along, you will discover some of the most incredible facts of the most published book in history. After we have tested the validity of the physical accuracy of the Bible, we can then examine the prophecies made, and you will discover that there is no book that has ever been penned in the history of the world that has the same perfect record concerning the predicting of historical events.

THE OLD TESTAMENT

There are only a few hundred manuscripts that we have for the Old Testament. The Old Testament track record of being duplicated by hand-written means is stunning when one is aware of the rigid laws governing the transcribing of the Scriptures. Samuel Davidson in the *Hebrew Text of the Old Testament* lists regimens that the Talmudists (A.D. 100–500) observed. Here follows a sampling:

1. An authentic copy must be the exemplar, from which the transcriber ought not in the least deviate
2. No word or letter, not even a yod, must be written from memory
3. Between every consonant the space of a hair or thread must intervene
4. Between every book, three lines
5. The copyist must sit in full Jewish dress
6. Wash his whole body
7. Not begin to write the name of God with a pen newly dipped in ink[44]

Between the seventh and tenth centuries B.C., Jewish scholars called Masoretes gathered primarily in Tiberias and developed an intricate system for transcribing the Old Testament, which has resulted in the standard Hebrew text used today. Below are a few of their meticulous rules for transcription:

1. Counted the number of times each letter in the alphabet occurs in each book
2. Numbered the verses, words, and letters of every book and calculate the middle letter of each
3. Pointed out the middle letter of the Pentateuch and the whole Hebrew Bible
    (It should be noted that these calculations were made and committed to memory by mnemonics and always checked against the original text.)[45]

Is it any wonder then that the Old Testament is almost a carbon copy of that which was originally penned? The discovery of the Dead Sea Scrolls in 1947 completely solidified the question of whether the scrolls had been precisely transmitted since the initial completion of the Old Testament in 400 B.C. The argument that persisted prior to this great discovery was this: Since the oldest manuscript that we have dates around A.D. 900, how do we know that the Old Testament was accurately transmitted since the time of Christ in A.D. 32? The Dead Sea Scrolls answered that question forever. The date of the writing of the different scrolls dates as early as 200 B.C. The Book of Isaiah, for example, is dated by paleographers around 125 B.C. The Dead Sea Scrolls confirmed the unprecedented accurate transmission of a document of antiquity over a period of 1000 years!

As the bibliographical test for the Old Testament has been passed with flying colors, let us take a look at the internal and external evidences that support the historical exactness of the Old Testament.

DR. WILSON, STAND AND TAKE A BOW

Modern archaeology has confirmed the accuracy of biblical reporting. An argument that persisted among liberal theologians was that Moses could not have written the first five books of the Old Testament—Genesis, Exodus, Leviticus, Numbers, and Deuteronomy—because there wasn't a written language in existence during the lifetime of Moses. This theory fell in 1974 when Dr. Paolo Matthiae, one of Italy's leading archaeologists, discovered the greatest archaeological find of the seventies: Ebla. At this find, located in northeast Syria between the cities of Ur and Aleppo, were discovered over *16,000* cuneiform tablets in several different languages which predated Moses by one thousand years! And the languages demonstrate the same degree of sophistication as the Old Testament text penned by Moses. Ebla also confirmed the actual existence of several key cities listed in the Old Testament that were thought to be fictitious. Two of these cities were Sodom and Gomorrah. In the tablets discovered, were economic transactions that showed Ebla was a powerful city and collected taxes from Sodom and Gomorrah—cities that many thought were invented in the Old Testament text to illustrate the serious consequences of what happens to a people when they turn from God. There are literally hundreds of other examples that could be quoted to demonstrate the astounding accuracy of the historical content of the Bible. We will examine one of these discoveries made by the amazing Dr. Robert Dick Wilson.

Born in 1886, in Pennsylvania, Dr. Wilson received his doctorate at the College of New Jersey, which later became known as Princeton University. He subsequently attended the University of Berlin, in Germany, and then taught Old Testament courses at Western Theological Seminary in Pittsburgh. When in Germany, Dr. Wilson made a decision. This is his own personal account. "I was twenty-five then; and I judged from the life of my ancestors that I would live to be seventy; so that I should have forty-five years to work. I divided the period into three parts. The first fifteen years I would devote to the study of the languages necessary. For the second fifteen I was going to devote myself to the study of the text of the Old Testament; and I reserved the last fifteen years for the work of writing the results of my previous studies and investigations so as to give them to the world."[46]

"Most of our students used to go to Germany, and they heard professors give lectures which were the results of their own labours. The students took everything because the professor said it. I went there to study so that there would be no professor on earth that could lay down the law for me, or say anything without my being able to investigate the evidence on which he said it."[47]

"Now I consider that what was necessary in order to investigate the evidence was, first of all, to know the languages in which the evidence is given. So I determined that I would learn all the languages that throw light upon the Hebrew, and also the languages into which the Bible had been translated down to A.D. 600, so that I could investigate the text myself."[48]

This statement was not a casual one for Dr. Wilson mastered forty-five languages and dialects in his first fifteen years! He was able to read the New Testament in nine different languages and had memorized a Hebrew translation of the New Testament text syllable for syllable! Dr. Walvoord, president of Dallas Theological Seminary, called Dr. Wilson "probably the outstanding authority on ancient languages of the Middle East."[49] Dr. Wilson's forty-five years of research led him to make the following conclusive statement, "I can affirm that there is not a page of the Old Testament concerning which we need have any doubt." What follows is an example unparalleled by any other document of antiquity for transmission over a period of over a thousand years of historical information.

Take the following case. There are twenty-nine ancient kings whose names are mentioned not only in the Bible but also on monuments of their own time; many of them under their own supervision. There are one hundred and ninety-five consonants in these twenty-nine proper names. Yet we find that in the documents of the Hebrew Old Testament there are only two or three out of the entire hundred and ninety-five about which there can be any question of their being written in exactly the same way as they were inscribed on their own monuments. Some of these go back for two thousand years, some for four thousand; and are so written that every letter is clear and correct. This is surely a wonder.

Compare this accuracy with that of other writings—take the list made by the greatest scholar of his age, the librarian at Alexandria in 200 B.C. He compiled a catalogue of the Kings of Egypt, thirty-eight in all; of the entire number only three or four of them are recognizable. He also made a list of the kings of Assyria; in only one case can we tell who is meant; and that one is not spelled correctly. Or take Ptolemy, who drew up a register of eighteen of the kings of Babylon. Not one of them is properly spelled; you could not make them out at all if you did not know from other sources to what he is referring. If any one talks against the Bible, ask him about the kings mentioned in it. There are twenty-nine kings of Egypt, Israel, Moab, Damascus, Tyre, Babylon, Assyria, and Persia, referred to and ten different countries among these twenty-nine; all of which are included in the Bible accounts and those of the monuments. Every one of these is given his right name in the Bible, his right country, and placed in the correct chronological order. Think what that means![50]

Thanks to Dr. Wilson's efforts, one can be assured beyond a reasonable doubt that the Bible is an astoundingly accurate document that is unmatched for the transmission of historic events when examined through either external or internal evidential proofs. For those seriously interested in other evidences confirmed through archaeological discoveries, I suggest consulting the Source Notes for this chapter.

WILL THE NEW TESTAMENT TAKE THE STAND?

As has been demonstrated through an examination of the evidence, the Old Testament is a trustworthy and sound historical document. If the Old Testament is not historically sound, then we would have no assurance that the predictions which will now be examined in the Old Testament were not changed down through the centuries. The New Testament has just as an astounding track record.

When applying the bibliographical test as earlier stated, we have over 24,000 manuscripts versus the *Iliad*'s 643. So, from a manuscript position alone, the New Testament has more manuscript authority than any ten pieces of classical literature of the same time period combined! What is even more striking is the time variance. There is a time lag of 500 years between the original text of the *Iliad* and the extant copy, while the New Testament dates about A.D. 80 or roughly 50 years after the historical events documented. William Albright states:

> In my opinion, every book of the New Testament was written by a baptized Jew between the forties and the eighties of the first A.D. (very probably sometime between about 50 and 75).[51]

We can conclude that the New Testament meets every requirement to pass a rigid bibliographical test. The historical accuracy of the New Testament can now be scrutinized for internal and external proofs.

Because of the short time span between the accounts detailed in the New Testament and their being written down and distributed, the writers had to be deadly accurate in their reporting, or critics could easily discredit the new Christian faith. The New Testament accounts of the life of Jesus and His teachings, for example, were written by men who were either eyewitnesses or who recorded eyewitness accounts of the events and teachings surrounding the life of Jesus of Nazareth.

Inasmuch as many have undertaken to compile an account of the things accomplished among us, just as those who from the beginning were eyewitnesses and servants of the Word have handed them down to us, it seemed fitting for me as well, having investigated everything carefully from the beginning, to write it out for you in consecutive order, most excellent Theophilus.

Luke 1:1-3 NAS

For we did not follow cleverly devised tales when we made known to you the power and coming of our Lord Jesus Christ, but we were eyewitnesses of His majesty.

2 Peter 1:16 NAS

Now in the fifteenth year of the reign of Tiberius Caesar, when Pontius Pilate was governor of Judea, and Herod was tetrarch of Galilee, and his brother Philip was tetrarch of the regions of Ituraea and Trachonitis, and Lysanias was tetrarch of Abilene.

Luke 3:1 NAS

If there were discrepancies of either an intentional or unintentional nature, there would have arisen statements from critics to set right the inaccuracies. Nothing has been found to make a significant case from contemporaries of the apostles.

The New Testament accounts of Christ were being circulated within the lifetimes of those alive at the time of His life. These people could certainly confirm or deny the accuracy of the accounts. In advocating their case for the gospel, the apostles had appealed (even when confronting their most severe opponents) to common knowledge concerning Jesus. They not only said, "Look, we saw this" or "We heard that ..." but they turned the tables around and right in front of adverse critics said, "You also know about these things ... You saw them; you yourselves know about it." One had better be careful when he says to his opposition, "You know this also." because if he isn't right in the details, it will be shoved right back down his throat.[52]

Acts 2:22 (NAS) illustrates this point:

Men of Israel, listen to these words: Jesus the Nazarene, a man attested to you by God with miracles and wonders and signs which God performed through Him in your midst, just as you yourselves know....

New Testament scholar Robert Grant of the University of Chicago concludes:

At the time they (the synoptic gospels) were written or may be supposed to have been written, there were eyewitnesses and their testimony was not completely disregarded.... This means that the gospels must be regarded as largely reliable witnesses to the life, death, and resurrection of Jesus."[53]

Will Durant, who was trained in the discipline of historical investigation, and spent his life analyzing records of antiquity, writes:

Despite the prejudices and theological preconceptions of the evangelist, they record many incidents that mere inventors would have concealed—the competition of the apostles for high places in the Kingdom, their flight after Jesus' arrest, Peter's denial, the failure of Christ to work miracles in Galilee, the references of failure of Christ to work miracles in Galilee, the references of some auditors to his possible insanity, his early uncertainty as to his mission, his confessions of ignorance as to the future, his moments of bitterness, his despairing cry on the cross; no one reading these scenes can doubt the reality of the figure behind them. That a few simple men should in one generation have invented so powerful and appealing a personality, so lofty an ethic, and so inspiring a vision of human brotherhood, would be a miracle far more incredible than any recorded in the Gospels. After two centuries of Higher Criticism the outlines of the life, character, and teaching of Christ remain reasonably clear, and constitute the most fascinating feature in the history of Western man.[54]

There is little doubt that the writers of the New Testament tried, in as fair and as straightforward a manner as possible, to put down the facts with the information that they had available to them. This information was derived from their own eyewitness accounts as well as the eyewitness accounts of others. Archaeological discoveries have consistently borne out the historical accuracy with which the events in the New Testament were detailed. The details of the circumstances surrounding the birth of Jesus are another example of sound historical documentation.

There was a time when scholars believed that Luke was inaccurate in detailing the events at the time of the birth of Christ. The argument persisted that: (1) there was no census; (2) Quirinius was not the governor of Syria; (3) everyone did not have to return to his ancestral home.

First of all, archaeological discoveries prove beyond a shadow of a doubt that the Romans had a regular enrollment of taxpayers and also held censuses every 14 years. This procedure was indeed begun under Augustus and the first took place in either 23–22 B.C. or in 9–8 B.C.

Secondly, we find evidence that Quirinius was governor of Syria around 7 B.C. This assumption is based on an incription found in Antioch ascribing to Quirinius this post. As a result of this finding, it is now supposed that he was governor twice. Once in 7 B.C. and the other time in A.D. 6.

Lastly, in regard to the practices of enrollment, a papyrus found in Egypt gives directions for the conduct of a census. It reads: "Because of the approaching census it is necessary that all those residing for any cause away from their homes should at once prepare to return to their own governments in order that they may complete the family registration of the enrollment and that the tilled lands may retain those belonging to them.[55]

Even under minute scrutiny the New Testament has an amazing track record concerning seemingly insignificant documentation.

> Also in doubt were Luke's usages of certain words. Luke refers to Philippi as a "part" or "district" of Macedonia. He uses the Greek word *meris* which is translated "part" or "district." F.J.A. Hort believed Luke wrong in this usage. He said that *meris* referred to a "portion" not a "district," thus, his grounds for disagreement. Archaeological excavations, however, have shown that this very word, *meris* was used to describe the divisions of the district. Thus, archaeology has again shown the accuracy of Luke.[56]

The stunning accuracy of Luke's account of the gospel caused a former skeptic of the New Testament's historical accuracy to recant his former opinions in light of key archaeological discoveries. Sir William Ramsay, one of the greatest archaeologists of all time wrote:

> Luke is an historian of the first rank ... this author should be placed along with the greatest of historians.[57]

Luke has demonstrated great accuracy in the recording of two books he has written in the New Testament. Norman L. Geisler and William E. Nix demonstrate an even greater accuracy, for the transmission of the entire New Testament in relationship to other works of antiquity when they conclude that:

> The New Testament has about 20,000 lines ...; the *Iliad* has about 15,000. Only 40 lines (or about 400 words) of the New Testament are in doubt whereas 764 lines of the *Iliad* are questioned. This 5 percent textual corruption compares with one-half of one percent of similar emendations in the New Testament.[58]

We have now established two axioms vital to the investigation of several specific biblical prophecies:

1. The predictions we will pursue can be categorically assumed to have been transmitted accurately due to the historical proofs provided and demonstrated.

2. We can also conclude that the historical events recorded in the New Testament are accurate due to the scrutiny of bibliographical, internal, and external proofs applied to the text.

Now let us examine the predictions in light of the evidence presented.

THE PREDICTIONS

For the better part of two thousand years prior to the birth of Jesus of Nazareth, the Jew looked for and anticipated the physical coming of the Messiah or Savior. The Old Testament is laced with over 60 major prophecies and 270 ramifications of how the Messiah would be born, live, and die, even the implications surrounding his life and death. It is common knowledge that when a Jewish prophet recorded a prophecy, he believed in a literal, historical fulfillment of that prediction. What follows are 8 predictions made by the Old Testament prophets hundreds of years before the birth of Christ.

PROPHECY #1

"Behold, the days are coming," declares the Lord,
"When I shall raise up for David a righteous Branch;
And He will reign as king and act wisely
And do justice and righteousness in the land ....
And this is His name by which He will be called,
'The Lord our righteousness."

Jeremiah 23:5, 6 NAS

RELEVANCE: Jeremiah, as did all the prophets, looked towards the coming of the Messiah. Jeremiah and other prophets made many prophecies concerning who the Messiah would be so that when He lived on earth men would know who He was through the revelation of the Lord's message rather than just one claiming to be the Messiah with no evidence to back his story. Here Jeremiah makes reference to the fact that the Messiah would be born out of the lineage of King David.

FULFILLMENT: Jesus was born out of the family line of David. Luke details the exact family lineage in Luke 3:23–38. Considering Luke's meticulous attention to details as earlier demonstrated and the fact that the family lineage has never been credibly contested, we may assume—based upon the historical proofs earlier applied—that Jesus was from the family lineage of King David.

PROPHECY #2

"But as for you, Bethlehem Ephrathah,
Too little to be among the clans of Judah,
From you One will go forth for Me to be ruler in Israel.
His goings forth are from long ago,
From the days of eternity."

Micah 5:2 NAS

RELEVANCE: Here the Prophet Micah tells of the birthplace of the Messiah. Notice that it is not just any king but one "whose goings forth are from long ago, from the days of eternity."
FULFILLMENT: Luke accounts for the location of Jesus' birth in Luke 2:4, 5 and 7 NAS.

And Joseph also went up from Galilee, from the city of Nazareth, to Judea, to the city of David, which is called Bethlehem, because he was of the house and family of David, in order to register, along with Mary, who was engaged to him, and was with child.... And she gave birth to her first-born son....

PROPHECY #3

"Behold, I am going to send My messenger, and he will clear the way before Me, And the Lord, whom you seek, will suddenly come to His temple; and the messenger of the covenant, in whom you delight, behold, He is coming," says the Lord of Hosts.

Malachi 3:1 NAS

RELEVANCE: Here the Prophet Malachi states there will be a forerunner who will precede the Messiah, one who will announce and prepare the people for His coming.

FULFILLMENT: John the Baptist was, of course, the one who prepared the way for Christ.

> Now in those days John the Baptist came, preaching in the wilderness of Judea, saying, "Repent, for the kingdom of heaven is at hand."
>
> Matthew 3:1, 2 NAS

PROPHECY #4

> ... But later on He shall make it glorious, by the way of the sea, on the other side of Jordan, Galilee of the Gentiles.
>
> Isaiah 9:1 NAS

RELEVANCE: The Prophet Isaiah is speaking of the Messiah and where his ministry would begin.

FULFILLMENT:

> Now when He heard that John had been taken into custody, He withdrew into Galilee; and leaving Nazareth, He came and settled in Capernaum, which is by the sea, in the region of Zebulun and Naphtali.
>
> From that time Jesus began to preach and say, "Repent; for the kingdom of heaven is at hand."
>
> Matthew 4:12, 13, 17 NAS

PROPHECY #5

> Even my close friend, in whom I trusted,
> Who ate my bread,
> Has lifted up his heel against me.
>
> Psalms 41:9 NAS

RELEVANCE: King David is referring to the time when the Messiah would be betrayed by a close friend. History would later record his name as Judas Iscariot.
FULFILLMENT:

> While He was still speaking, behold, a multitude came, and the one called Judas, one of the twelve, was preceding them; and he approached Jesus to kiss Him. But Jesus said to him, "Judas, are you betraying the Son of Man with a kiss?"
>
> Luke 22:47, 48 NAS

PROPHECY #6

> And I said to them, "If it is good in your sight, give me my wages; but if not, never mind!" So they weighed out thirty shekels of silver as my wages.
>
> Zechariah 11:12 NAS

RELEVANCE: Zechariah states that the price to be paid for the betrayal of the Messiah would be thirty pieces of silver.
FULFILLMENT:

> And said unto them, What will ye give me, and I will deliver him unto you? And they covenanted with him for thirty pieces of silver.
>
> Matthew 26:15

Here Matthew recounts that Judas was paid thirty pieces of silver to betray Jesus. Zechariah 11:13 further states two other incidents that would surround the betrayal. ". . . So I took the thirty shekels of silver and threw them to the potter in the house of the Lord" Matthew reports in Matthew 27:5-7 that Judas took and threw the money into the sanctuary and that the money was then picked up by the chief priests and was used to buy a potter's field. This was done because it was unlawful to take "blood money" and place in the treasury. This gives us seven ramifications that were fulfilled around these two prophecies.

1. Betrayal
2. By a friend
3. For 30 pieces (not 29)
4. Silver
5. Thrown down (not placed)
6. In the House of the Lord
7. Money used to buy potter's field[59]

PROPHECY #7

His grave was assigned to be with wicked men, Yet with a rich man in His death....

Isaiah 53:9 NAS

RELEVANCE: Isaiah plainly states that the Messiah would be buried in a rich man's tomb.
FULFILLMENT:

... there came a rich man from Arimathea, named Joseph.... and asked for the body of Jesus.... And Joseph took the body and wrapped it in a clean linen cloth, and laid it in his own new tomb ....

Matthew 27:57–60 NAS

Luke detailed the same account of the burial of Jesus in Luke 23:50–53.

PROPHECY #8

... They pierced my hands and my feet.

Psalms 22:16

And I will pour upon the house of David, and upon the inhabitants of Jerusalem, the spirit of grace and of supplications; and they shall look upon me whom they have pierced, and they shall mourn for him, as one mourneth for his only son, and shall be in bitterness for him, as one that is in bitterness for his firstborn.

Zechariah 12:10

And one shall say unto him, What are these wounds in thine hands?
Then he shall answer, "Those with which I was wounded in the house
of my friends."

Zechariah 13:6

RELEVANCE: This is perhaps the most stunning of all prophecies.
Death for the Messiah is clearly delineated through the piercing of
the hands and feet as stated by King David roughly eight or nine
hundred years before the birth of Jesus and the prophecy of
Zechariah dates approximately 450 years before the birth of Christ.
What is remarkable is that both men were describing the penalty of
death by crucifixion. Crucifixion wasn't even in existence at the time
either David or Zechariah made his prophecies! The first time
crucifixion was used in Israel was approximately sixty years before
Jesus was born.

THE PROBABILITY FACTORS

One might argue that the prophecies stated have been fulfilled in
other men. Maybe one or two of the prophecies have but not the
eight just detailed. Peter Stoner wrote a treatise called *Science
Speaks*. In it he illustrates the odds necessary for the eight
prophecies to be fulfilled in one man's life. The manuscript was then
sent to H. Harold Hartzler, of the American Scientific Affiliation. Mr.
Hartzler in the foreword to *Science Speaks* states:

The manuscript for *Science Speaks* has been carefully reviewed by a
committee of the American Scientific Affiliation members and by the
Executive Council of the same group and has been found, in general,
to be dependable and accurate in regard to the scientific material
presented. The mathematical analysis included is based upon
principles of probability which are thoroughly sound, and Professor
Stoner has applied these principles in a proper and convincing way.[60]

Mr. Stoner states that we find that the chance that any man might
have lived down to the present time and fulfilled all eight prophecies
is 1 in 10^{17}. That means that if you were a betting person you would

have 1 chance out of 100,000,000,000,000,000 for eight prophecies to be fulfilled in one man's life. To make this a little more graphic, Mr. Stoner asks us to imagine that:

> We take 10^{17} silver dollars and lay them on the face of Texas. They will cover all of the state two feet deep. Now mark one of these silver dollars and stir the whole mass thoroughly, all over the state. Blindfold a man and tell him that he can travel as far as he wishes, but he must pick up one silver dollar and say that this is the right one. What chance would he have of getting the right one? Just the same chance the prophets would have had of writing these eight prophecies and having them all come true in any one man, from their time to the present time.[61]

It is rather obvious to any thinking person that the prophecies and their fulfillment in the life of Christ are no coincidence. And we have only examined eight of the prophecies. If we apply the probability test to just 48 of the prophecies which Christ fulfilled, the probability factor jumps up to 1 chance in 10^{157}—that is a 1 followed by 157 zeroes for those of you who have been out of school for a while. The science of mathematics, rather than scarring the prophecies, elevates them to a higher level of credibility. It also cannot be argued that the New Testament writers made the script fit the prophecies, because of the historical accuracy with which the writers recorded the gospels.

If the writers fictitiously created the life of Christ, there is nothing to suggest this in the 24,000 manuscripts discovered. It would have required a humanly impossible effort to get all the manuscripts written by different writers to match up to the same fraudulent story.

Another explanation that might be given is that Jesus deliberately orchestrated the events in His life so that they would match up to the 60 prophecies and over 270 ramifications detailing the life of the Messiah to come. This was not possible, however, because Jesus could not determine his place of birth, his family lineage, and so forth. Even if he could, by the law of statistics this is considered impossible. Dr. Duane Tolbert Gish, who received his Ph.D. in biochemistry at the University of California and served on the research staff of the

Upjohn Company, one of the nation's largest pharmaceutical firms, states that when one deals with a probability factor of 10^{17} power or higher—from a scientific viewpoint—it is considered impossible. To say that Jesus could have controlled the family lineage, place of birth, the area He would begin His ministry, being preceded by a forerunner, betrayal by a friend for thirty pieces of silver, burial in a rich man's tomb, and death by crucifixion, is considered mathematically and scientifically impossible.

FRAUD AN IMPOSSIBILITY

A hard-and-fast case was first made for the reliability of the historical and transmissional accuracy of the Bible. Eight Old Testament prophecies that were made hundreds of years before the events had taken place have been illustrated. One cannot say that the Old Testament prophecies were changed after the birth of Christ because this contradicts the historical proofs earlier stated. The Old Testament as we have it today is the same as recorded by the Old Testament writers.

I initially stated that I would make a case for the supernatural based upon facts rather than a particular philosophic bent. If the Bible is indeed the Word of God as the prophets claim, then their predictions for the future should be just as valid. What follows are just a few of the stunning prophecies that it appears we are seeing fulfilled in our lifetime.

As stated earlier, the reason biblical prophecy has been chosen to make a case for the supernatural is that it can be analyzed impartially. Either the events come to pass or they do not. The prophets made many predictions other than those dealing with the coming of the Messiah. One area of particular interest today is that of the events that are to take place before the return of Christ.

CURRENT PROPHECIES

For many, the current focusing of world power in the Middle East appears to be a direct fulfillment of prophecies made as long as 2600 years ago. Dr. John F. Walvoord, a recognized authority in the field of biblical eschatology and president of Dallas Theological Seminary, published a book in 1974 entitled, *Armageddon, Oil and the Middle East Crisis*, which he wrote with John E. Walvoord. In this well-written treatise, he depicted the rapid fulfillment of biblical prophecy in the Middle East. It is written in a highly responsible manner and not written for the sake of putting another sensational book about prophecy on the market. It is recommended reading regardless of whether one espouses Christian beliefs or not. Since its publication in 1974, it has been amazing to see how accurate Dr. Walvoord was in his analysis of the prophecies against the backdrop of current events in the Middle East.

The conservative Christian camp believes that the return of Christ is close at hand. It can, of course, be argued that Christians of every generation have believed their generation would be the one to see Christ return. For those not familiar with the events according to the prophets that will surround the return of Christ, Dr. Walvoord's book is highly recommended. Five of these prophecies have been selected to allow the reader to realize just how accurate the prophets were in their prognostications. All five of the prophecies detailed were probably looked upon as being obviously allegorical in nature even as little as two or three hundred years ago. But the perspective of the prophets was a literal one.

Remember that the prophets expected an actual historical fulfillment of the prophecies. Their perspective was this: If the Lord they served and worshiped could bring about such great miracles as the splitting of the Red Sea and prevent Shadrach, Meshach, and Abednego from being incinerated in Nebuchadnezzar's furnace, then why wouldn't the revelation from the Lord dealing with the future be historically fulfilled?

PROPHECY #1

They led an army of 200,000,000 warriors—I heard an announcement of how many there were.

Revelation 9:16 LB

RELEVANCE: The Apostle John, exiled on the Isle of Patmos around the year A.D. 81, states that in the end times, there would be an army of two hundred million men that would war on Israel. When John penned this prophecy, there were not that many people living on the face of the earth! For centuries, many scholars mused that the figure was allegorical and did not require serious inspection. On April 24, 1964, Associated Press stated that in 1961 there were approximately 200,000,000 armed militiamen in the communist country of China.

PROPHECY #2

And the word of the Lord came to me saying, "Son of man, set your face toward Gog of the land of Magog. . . . Therefore, prophesy, son of man, and say to Gog. . . . "And you will come from your place out of the remote parts of the north, you and many peoples with you, all of them riding on horses, a great assembly and a mighty army; and you will come up against My people Israel. . . ."

Ezekiel 38:1, 2, 14, 15, 16 NAS

And I will turn thee back, and leave but the sixth part of thee . . . And I will smite thy bow out of thy left hand, and will cause thine arrows to fall out of thy right hand. . . . And it shall come to pass in that day, that I will give unto Gog a place there of graves in Israel, the valley of the passengers on the east of the sea: and it shall stop the noses of the passengers: and there shall they bury Gog and all his multitude: and they shall call it the valley of Hamongog. And seven months shall the house of Israel be burying of them, that they may cleanse the land.

Ezekiel 39:2, 3, 11, 12

RELEVANCE: Historians have traced back the ancestry of the Russians and the people of Magog are their ancestors. What Ezekiel is prophesying is the invasion of the land of Israel by the Russians. This prediction would have been considered preposterous as little as 100 years ago because Israel was not a nation. As others have commented, the Middle East crisis appears to be moving in a direction towards the direct fulfilling of this prophecy as the Russians move to control the Persian Gulf region. It is no secret that there is open hatred from the USSR toward Israel.

PROPHECY #3

> For the Lord has a day of vengeance,
> A year of recompense for the cause of Zion.
> And its streams shall be turned into pitch,
> And its loose earth into brimstone,
> And its land shall become burning pitch.
> It shall not be quenched night or day. . . .

Isaiah 34:8–10 NAS

RELEVANCE: In these verses Isaiah is speaking of something that will take place in the end times. With the current fulcrum of power centered in the Middle East due to the fact that the majority of the world's oil supply comes from this region, it is interesting that Isaiah states that the land shall be turned into burning pitch. This could never have happened until oil was discovered and production started. The Arab nations have stated that before they would allow their countries with their oil fields to be taken over by a foreign power, they would sabotage those fields.

PROPHECY #4

> Behold, a day is coming for the Lord when the spoil taken from you will be divided among you. For I will gather all the nations against Jerusalem to battle, and the city will be captured, the houses plundered, the women ravished, and half of the city exiled, but the rest of the people will not be cut off from the city. Then the Lord will go forth and fight against those nations, as when He fights on a day of battle. And in that day His feet will stand on the Mount of Olives, which is in front of Jerusalem on the east; and the Mount of Olives will be split in its middle from east to west by a very large valley, so that half of the mountain will move toward the north and the other half toward the south.

Zechariah 14:1–4 NAS

RELEVANCE: Zechariah, the prophet, is speaking of the end times before the Messiah shall return and reign in power. It is interesting that the prophet states that half of the inhabitants of Jerusalem will be exiled. Jerusalem today is split in two sections. The west side is Israeli, and the east side is Arab. It is the guess of many scholars that the Jews will be exiled to one half of the city. But even more stunning is that the Prophet Zechariah described a strike-slip earthquake with half of the Mount of Olives moving north and the other half to the south. There is no way that Zechariah could have known that there was a geological fault through the Mount of Olives, because geologists did not know this until 1976 when a survey of the Mount of Olives was made by Hunt Oil. Amos Nur of the department of geophysics of Stanford University presented a paper to the annual meeting of the American Geophysical Union concerning earthquake activity where the Arabic and African plates meet in Israel. He stated that the data confirmed that "The east side (Arabic plate) is slipping north relative to the west side (Africa plate) at a rate of about .5 meters per quake." Continuing, he added, "it is amazing that Zechariah chose to describe strike-slip motion."[62]

PROPHECY #5

For then there will be a great tribulation, such as has not occurred since the beginning of the world until now, nor ever shall. And unless those days had been cut short, no life would have been saved; but for the sake of the elect those days shall be cut short.

Matthew 24:21, 22 NAS

RELEVANCE: Jesus was in the Temple in Jerusalem speaking to His disciples concerning those things that would take place before His return. He told the disciples that unless He returned mankind would be utterly destroyed. The threat of total destruction due to nuclear holocaust is a cold, hard fact of life today. For the Christian these words of Christ are a great source of encouragement. For those who do not espouse a belief in Christ, this prophecy may be lightly regarded or reacted to with fear. When the Rapture (for a description of this event see Dr. Walvoord's book) occurs, however, these individuals are going to be hard pressed for some logical and scientific answers. "Probably the work of some UFOs" will be their reply.

CONCLUDING REMARKS

Dr. Sagan issued forth the legitimate challenge for "compelling evidence." The Messianic prophecies certainly call for a further consideration and study of the claims of Christ. The prophecies concerning the future will cause one to evaluate these events as they are historically fulfilled. The science of archaeology has not "scarred" the validity of biblical prophecy. To the contrary, it has been the pivotal point for modern man's ability to substantiate the validity of prophecy. If the Bible is true to its word, as we believe it is, it would be futile to scientifically prove all supernatural manifestations of the Lord. If He is infinite as the Scripture plainly states, then so are the possibilities of His manifestations. There is also no clear-cut assurance that with a finite mind one can even approach the nature, let alone the mind, of God and the full scope of His creation.

Harry Reasoner, the prominent news commentator for the popular CBS News show "60 Minutes," had this to say concerning Christ and what he called this "divine insanity." (The following excerpt is © CBS Inc. 1979. All Rights Reserved. Originally broadcast December 23, 1979 over the CBS Television Network as part of the program series.)

> Eleven years ago, in my previous incarnation on this broadcast, I did a little Christmas piece. It seemed like a good idea to repeat it. The basis for this tremendous annual burst of buying things and gift-giving and parties and near hysteria is a quiet event that Christians believe actually happened a long time ago. You can say that in all societies there's always been a mid-winter festival, and that many of the trappings of our Christmas are almost violently pagan; but you come

back to the central fact of the day in the quietness of Christmas morning—the birth of God on Earth.

It leaves you with only three ways of accepting Christmas: one is cynically, as a time to make money or endorse the making of it; one is graciously, the appropriate attitude for non-Christians, who wish their Christian fellow citizens all the joys to which their beliefs entitle them; and the third, of course, is reverently. If this is an anniversary of the appearance of the Lord of the universe in the form of a helpless baby, it is a very important day.

It's a startling idea, of course. My guess is that the whole story—that a virgin was selected by God to bear his Son as a way of showing his love and concern for man—it's my guess that in spite of all the lip service they have given it, it is not an idea that has been popular with theologians. It's a somewhat illogical idea, and theologians love logic almost as much as they love God. It's so revolutionary a thought that it probably could only come from a God who is beyond logic and beyond theology. It has a magnificent appeal. Almost nobody has seen God and almost nobody has any real idea of what He's like; and the truth is that among men the idea of seeing God suddenly and standing in the very bright light is not necessarily a completely comfortable and appealing idea.

But everybody has seen babies, and most people like them. If God wanted to be loved as well as feared, He moved correctly here. If He wanted to know His people, as well as rule them, He moved correctly here, for a baby growing up learns all about people. If God wanted to be intimately a part of man, He moved correctly, for the experience of birth and familyhood is our most intimate and precious experience.

So it comes beyond logic. It is either all falsehood, or it is the truest thing in the world. It is a story of the great innocence of God the baby, God in the power of man; and it is such a dramatic shot toward the heart that it—if it is not true, for Christians nothing is true.

So, if a Christian is touched only once a year, the touching is still worth it. And maybe on some given Christmas, some final quiet morning, the touch will take.

Danny Korem

PSYCHIATRIC COMMENT ON APOLOGETICS SECTION

At the age of twenty-two, I was a budding young scientist, acquiring an M.S. degree in cardiovascular physiology at Michigan State University. I was well disciplined in the scientific method and didn't take anything unprovable for granted. I was an evangelical Christian, but I was going through many personal doubts about whether Christianity was really any more true than other religions. I studied the other world religions and used logic to the best of my ability to come to the truth, realizing my own prejudices. When I studied and discovered the phenomenal accuracy of Bible prophecy and the historical evidence that these phenomenal Old Testament predictions were not written "after the fact," I became convinced that Christ really is God and that the Bible really is reliable. My temporarily shaky faith in Christ became solidified. Since those days I have come to believe that a degree of doubt, followed by solidification, is a healthy growth process that has taken place in nearly all of the committed Christians I know today. It is particularly common in adolescence. It takes a great deal of denial of reality for an educated person who has studied Bible prophecy in an objective fashion to deny that Christ is God. To deny Christ's deity would take a great deal of "faith" (misguided faith) for such a person.

Paul Meier, M.D.

13
Introduction to Demons and Angels

A case for the supernatural has been made from a biblical perspective because I have never found another reliable source either from the area of science or philosophy that has the integrity and historical validity as the Bible. For this reason, a strong point-by-point case was made for the physical reliability of the Bible as a historical document. If the recorded events are accurate, then the prophecies can be validated. The Bible also addresses many other areas of a supernatural nature. Among these are angels and demons.

This section of the text will deal with the proper understanding of one of the most interesting creatures that has ever confronted man. It will involve a study of angels: those that serve God and those that serve Satan. The relationship angels have with man is extremely important since they are able to communicate a lot about man's relationship to the supernatural and to his Creator. The theological terms denoting the study of angels and demons are *angelology* and *demonology*. We take the position that both groups are angels; therefore, to distinguish between these two groups of angels, the terms *angels* and *demons* (fallen angels) will be applied.

Several years ago, if the subject of demons or angels had been mentioned to me in a context that they actually existed, or if it was even suggested that they were operating today, I would have thought this line of thought absurd. I did believe that Jesus was the Messiah, the Savior. Raised as a Jew and having attended Hebrew school for several years during my youth, I was taught that Jesus was not the Messiah our people have so long awaited. When studying the messianic prophecies in the Old Testament, prophecies dealing with the coming of the Messiah as detailed in the last section, it became apparent to me that Jesus was the Messiah. I came to this realization approximately ten years ago and a rabbi with whom I conferred agreed with my decision and rationale. I am still a Jew, but a Jew who believes, based upon the biblical prophecies, that Jesus of Nazareth is the Messiah. I am called a Messianic Jew, as I still follow many of the beliefs of my heritage.

While I believed in the supernatural claims of Christ, as do millions of others in this country, and in the possibility of God intervening supernaturally in the flow of human events, I did not and would not consider the possibility of angels and demons in the same factual context that I considered biblical prophecy. This was largely due to the media and entertainment coverage in the areas of demonic and angelic activity. The manner in which demons and angels are portrayed to the public leaves a great deal to be desired. I found priests ranting and raving around a room with a cross in one hand and a flask of holy water in the other warding off evil spirits as amusing as Superman thrusting out his chest to stop speeding bullets. Had a legitimate presentation been made of demons and angels, their powers and realms of influence, earlier in my life, it might not have taken me as long to come to grips with their reality.

Demonstrating the legitimacy of biblical claims that angels and demons do exist to a world that discredits the reality of God is very difficult. I have personally investigated scores of cases where an individual claimed that demonic or angelic influences might be present. After examining the credibility of the witness or witnesses, their testimony, and the legitimacy of the events described, it is nearly impossible to "prove" scientifically that an angel or demon physically interrupted daily life. While *I personally believe* in their existence, although I have never personally encountered either, it has not been an easy task to *prove* their existence. Physical phenomena and phenomena of a psychological and psychiatric nature must be taken into consideration before a case is airtight.

Professor Walt Baker, associate professor of missions at Dallas Theological Seminary, told me of a case he personally encountered while in Haiti. For many years Professor Baker has studied and also witnessed firsthand the voodoo rites and cultic practices in that area of the world. He is considered a leading expert. One evening he received a call about a young woman, who had just killed her infant, who was thought to be demonically possessed. Professor Baker, while believing in the supernatural element, also carries a healthy skepticism of labeling something a manifestation of supernatural powers. After carefully considering the case, he convinced the relatives to allow him to take the young woman to a medical clinic, where it was discovered that she suffered from a chemical deficiency that caused her to lapse into a trancelike state. It was during this state that she killed her child by suffocation. Once the chemical imbalance was treated and psychiatric care administered to help the young woman with her guilt over what she had done, she was able to lead a normal and healthy life. One must exercise great caution when making judgments concerning the intervention of supernatural agents in day-to-day experiences.

The key word is *balance.* If one possesses a solid background of both the occult and the pseudo-occult, correct evaluations can be made and positive corrective action taken. It is our intention to make a statement concerning the demonic and angelic question in a nonsensationalized manner. As we examine both, background information will be supplied concerning the nature, powers, and the realm of influence of each according to the Scriptures. Lastly, a statement will be made as to how we as human beings are to respond to their activity.

DEMONS

Pursuing the question of demons requires that we begin with Lucifer. If you do not recognize his name, it is because his name was changed to Satan when he fell from his state of perfection. Scripture tells us that he was created the most beautiful and powerful of all the angels.

Again the word of the Lord came to me saying, "Son of man, take up a lamentation over the king of Tyre, and say to him, 'Thus says the Lord

God. "You had the seal of perfection. Full of wisdom and perfect in beauty. You were in Eden, the garden of God; Every precious stone was your covering: The ruby, the topaz, and the diamond; The beryl, the onyx, and the jasper; The lapis lazuli, the turquoise, and the emerald; And the gold, the workmanship of your settings and sockets, Was in you. On the day you were created They were prepared. You were the anointed cherub who covers, And I placed you there. You were on the holy mountain of God; You walked in the midst of the stones of fire. You were blameless in your ways From the day you were created, Until unrighteousness was found in you. By the abundance of your trade You were internally filled with violence, And you sinned; Therefore I have cast you as profane From the mountain of God. And I have destroyed you, O covering cherub, From the midst of the stones of fire. Your heart was lifted up because of your beauty; You corrupted your wisdom by reason of your splendor. I cast you to the ground; I put you before kings, That they may see you. By the multitude of your iniquities, In the unrighteousness of your trade, You profaned your sanctuaries. Therefore I have brought a fire from the midst of you; It has consumed you, And I have turned you to ashes on the earth In the eyes of all who see you. All who know you among the peoples Are appalled at you; You have become terrified, And you will be no more.'"

Ezekiel 28:11–19 NAS

In this long passage, Satan is represented as the king of Tyre by Bible scholars. This is because all the kingdoms of the world have been given to Satan as a result of the Fall of Man, which took place in the Garden of Eden. This authority of Satan's is recognized by God in the temptation of Jesus (see Matthew 4:8, 9; 2 Corinthians 4:4). Satan offered Jesus all the kingdoms of the world if only He would worship him. This passage from the book of Ezekiel also gives us a picture of Satan before his fall. Verse 14 calls Satan the "anointed cherub" which is Hebrew for the highest angel. He was beautiful and blameless. Even Satan's former name, *Lucifer,* means beauty: "the shining one."

The second passage of Scripture known to contain an account of the fall of Lucifer is Isaiah 14:12–15 (NAS):

> How you have fallen from heaven, O star of the morning, son of the dawn!… You who have weakened the nations! But you said in your heart, "I will ascend to heaven; I will raise my throne above the stars of God, And I will sit on the mount of assembly In the recesses of the north. I will ascend above the heights of the clouds; I will make myself like the Most High." Nevertheless you will be thrust down to Sheol, To the recesses of the pit.

In the five "I wills," Lucifer wrongfully desired to set his throne above the God who created him. While Satan was created perfect as was man, he was given the freedom of choice to either serve or not serve the Lord. When he made his rebellious decision, many other angels joined him and were subsequently thrown out of heaven. This sounds like the beginning of a fairy tale, but according to the scriptural record it is true. We must not fall into the trap of merely dispelling the account because it sounds too fantastic. The creation of the universe also has the same farfetched sort of a ring, but the creation of the universe is acknowledged regardless of whether one believes that a supernatural God in heaven created it or not.

When Lucifer and a host of angels "fell," most assume that they had taken on a hideous appearance. While Satan and his host are evil, there is no indication that they have lost any of their original beauty. In fact, 2 Corinthians 11:13, 14 tells us that Satan and his servants disguise themselves as "angels of light" and "servants of righteousness." Satan is the master of deception. Jesus called Satan the "father of lies" in John 8:44 and said "there is no truth in him." He is the con man's con. He has been at war with every good thing God and man have pursued. The very name *Satan* means "the adversary." Many may dismiss the concept of Satan and the fallen angels as mythology or present the devil as some nonpersonal evil force. But the Scriptures clearly teach that Satan is a real and personal being and that he, as well as his forces, is extremely powerful. His demons have all the powers of the Lord's angels—the only difference lying in the master they serve.

MISSION IMPOSSIBLE

Satan has only one goal for his pitiful existence, and it is to thwart the plans of God. He and his legion will go to great extremes to prevent an individual from gaining knowledge of who Jesus of Nazareth really is and what our relationship with Him should be. These truths are what he is out to destroy. I realize for some this will sound like a sermon, but there is no other way to accurately make this statement. The recent movies *Omen* and *Damien II* gave a Hollywood portrayal of who and what the Antichrist will be like. It is a mild portrayal in contrast to the biblical account. The Antichrist will be one whom Satan will totally indwell. He will first appear to be a great political leader who will solve many of the world's problems in the first three and a half years after Christ takes the Christians off the face of the Earth (the Rapture). In the last three and a half years, he will unleash the most terrible carnage the human race has ever seen. If this comes true as the Bible predicts, remember that it is Satan who has masterminded the scenario. For a human being without supernatural powers at his disposal to combat this kind of evil, the picture is not a bright one. It is upon this fear that Satan manipulates and moves. I have been told more than once by those who have been involved in organized crime that fear has been their greatest weapon. That fear can become an infinitely more immobilizing fear when a supernatural element is added.

As stated earlier, demons possess the same powers as angels. The list included demonstrates the powers that the biblical text depicts as peculiar to demons. When I am fielding questions at a lecture, the questioning always turns to the possibiity of demonic possession. That is the indwelling of a demon or Satan in a person. The possibility of possession does exist and is real; however, this area of activity is seldom if ever used by the "other side" as it is not very effective because of its visibility. It is too easy to identify a physical manifestation of a supernatural nature when it is performed out in the open. As stated earlier, Satan is the master of deception. As a magician I can vouch for the fact that the best way to fool an audience is to use a method of trickery that is far removed from what a spectator may surmise is the modus operandi. If all magicians hid objects up their sleeves, utilized mirrors, and trapdoors, our profession would have died many years ago. Who would go to pay good money to see a mystery if one already knew the answer? Satan would have become ineffective long ago if the majority of his activity was limited to possessing and scaring the daylights out of the human race. Logic dictates that the populace would immediately run to the Creator as the Bible states that the Lord has absolute and total authority over Satan and his legion. C. S. Lewis shrewdly depicts the working of the "legion" in *The Screwtape Letters*. It is highly recommended reading. Mr. Lewis catches the heart of satanic work as it moves to unravel family, church, and government, and describes how the attack is a well-balanced one. The story is told in the form of letters to a young demon and is particularly enlightening for those of an intellectual and nonchurch background. Mr. Lewis, once an atheist, is considered one of the great thinkers of this century.

In this sample passage from *The Screwtape Letters*, Screwtape is writing advice to Wormwood, one of his underlings:

I wonder you should ask me whether it is essential to keep the patient in ignorance of your own existence. That question, at least for the present phase of the struggle, has been answered for us by the high command. Our policy, for the moment, is to conceal ourselves. Of course this has not always been so. We are really faced with a cruel dilemma. When the humans disbelieve in our existence we lose all the pleasing results of direct terrorism. On the other hand, when they believe in us, we cannot make them materialists and sceptics. At least, not yet. I have great hopes that we shall learn in due time how to emotionalise and mythologise their science to such an extent that what is, in effect, a belief in us (though not under that name) will creep in while the human mind remains closed to belief in the Enemy. The "Life Force", the worship of sex, and some aspects of Psychoanalysis may here prove useful. If once we can produce our perfect work.... the man, not using, but veritably worshipping, what he vaguely calls "Forces" while denying the existence of "spirits"—then our final victory will be in sight. But in the meantime we must obey our orders. I do not think you will have much difficulty in keeping the patient in the dark. The fact that "devils" are predominantly *comic* figures in the modern imagination will help you. If any faint suspicion of your existence begins to arise in his mind, suggest to him a picture of something in red tights and persuade him that since he cannot believe in that (it is an old textbook method of confusing them) he therefore cannot believe in you.[63]

One area of pursuit that has been sadly neglected by most writers is the use of the pseudo-occult for the furthering of Satan's goal.

AND FOR MY NEXT TRICK ...

In the first half of the book we took a look at phenomena that most people believe are of a supernatural nature. We categorically demonstrated that all are brought about by physical or psychological means with a little luck added in for a key prediction or two, compliments of the neighborhood soothsayer. All of the pseudo-occultic phenomena detailed earlier can be used, however, from a satanic perspective.

Os Guiness in his book, *Encircling Eyes*, states that all phenomena relating to the study of the occult can be broken down into either those which are perpetrated by hoax or those which are genuine. This is partially true. Fire walking, however is neither a demonstration of a hoax nor a manifestation of a supernatural power. It is a scientific fact that man can walk across a bed of coals and not be burned. Hence, it falls into the area of the pseudo-occult or that which *appears* to be of a supernatural nature. Mr. Guiness later states that there are three possible answers for genuine phenomena. They are: (1) purely psychological power and knowledge, (2) supernatural power from Satan, (3) supernatural power from God. Mr. Guiness leaves no room for physical phenomena such as fire walking and muscle reading. He states that it is difficult to draw lines to separate these three areas. This is because Satan and his demons can counterfeit their own powers. In the thirteenth chapter of the Book of Revelation, it is predicted that the

Antichrist will be slain and then brought back to life. If we assume that this is true and Satan can bring the one he possesses back to life, then why aren't there cases of coal and fire handling that can match the feat of reviving a dead corpse? For example, why doesn't Satan allow participants to hold hot coals for extended periods, say one or two hours at a time? The reason is a simple one. Why use the real stuff if it isn't needed? The real purpose of fire walking, from Satan's perspective, is to further superstition and cultic practices that in and of themselves cause people to move in a direction away from God and His plan for their lives. This is the reason such practices are looked upon by the Lord as an abomination as stated in Deuteronomy 18:10. It is for this reason that I never encourage the experimenting with pseudo-occult phenomena. It causes a person to think that he or she has the power to manipulate matter, find the hidden well, prognosticate some future event, and so forth. It is a very cleverly played con game which Satan engages in. If he can make a person *think* that he has a power, in his mind it is the same as if he *has* the power. This is why the Bible refers to these practices as foolishness. A Christian need not have fear of any pseudo-occultic phenomenon except for its ability to draw an individual away from God.

SOME CONCLUSIONS

Recently, a book called *The Amityville Horror* made headlines as it was advertised as a true story about a house that was demonically "possessed." The concept seemed absurd, but because of the large number of questions concerning this case that came up during my lectures, I decided to do some research on the case. My findings confirmed that it was indeed a hoax, and a year later a national television show supported my conclusions. As stated in chapter 10, spirits of the dead cannot come back, because of spiritual laws the Lord has set up. Demons, while they can manipulate matter, do not possess houses. Every haunted-house story that has made newspaper headlines has been debunked. Milbourne Christopher has exposed many of these cases himself. Yet many people still believe haunted houses exist. So why should demons do the real thing, when people will swallow shallow stories like *The Amityville Horror?*

If one is a Christian, one need not have any fear of the demonic, because a Christian has complete and absolute authority over Satan and his legion through the power of Christ. It is not holy water and a properly held cross that convey the power of exorcism, as suggested by the media and purported exorcists. Rather, it is the power of Jesus Christ. In the sixteenth chapter of the Book of Acts, vv. 16–18, we have an example in which the Apostle Paul cast out a demon of divination from a woman by saying nothing more than, "'I command thee in the name of Jesus Christ to come out of her.' And he came out the same hour." Please note that there were no Gothic ceremonies performed. It was merely with the authority of Christ that the demons came out. This passage raises another question. Can demons predict the future as this passage seems to suggest?

In these verses one might get the impression that the woman, via the demon, could predict the future as the text states, ". . . a certain damsel possessed with a spirit of divination met us, which brought her masters much gain by soothsaying. . . . And when her masters saw the hope of their gains was gone, they caught Paul and Silas, and drew them into the marketplace unto the rulers" (vv. 16, 19). It is clear that these merchants were upset because their profits were dwindling due to the loss of the "spirit of divination." Demons do not have the power to predict future events with 100 percent accuracy. Angels were never given this power. However, since demons are scattered all over the face of the earth it can be speculated that they would have more timely knowledge than man, simply because they can see what is going on in many parts of the world simultaneously and know what secret decisions men make. Drawing on this knowledge plus their knowledge of human nature, one can imagine how demons predict future events with a degree of accuracy. I must admit, however, that I have never met one who had been given this power nor have I ever heard of a case where it was demonstrated. The few possible cases that have been brought to my attention were all easily attributed either to cold reading or pure luck.

In this short discourse on demons, we have tried to point out the fact to the reader that most phenomena are not a product of direct demonic intervention and that the Christian through Christ has authority over the demon when direct intervention occurs. This is not to say that Satan and his legion are not active, but rather, as suggested by C. S. Lewis, their objectives and methods are far more deadly because of their subtlety.

PSYCHIATRIC COMMENT ON DEMONS

I began an extensive study of demonology while still in medical school, because I decided to go into psychiatry. I thought I would have to differentiate between patients with psychological conflicts and demon-possessed individuals. I have studied every Bible passage that has anything to do with demonic activity. I have spent hours talking to missionaries from various countries. I read books on demonology, most of which are naively dramatic. I even attended a conference on demonology at Notre Dame, attended by Christian psychiatrists, seminary professors, and missionaries from all over the world. After years of studying demonology and looking for demon possession in my thousands of patients, I can honestly say that I have never yet seen a single case of demon possession. The main thing I have learned about demon possession is how little we really know about it and how little the Bible really says about it.

I have had hundreds of patients who came to see me because they thought they were demon possessed. Scores of them heard "demon voices" telling them evil things to do. It was at first surprising to me that all of these had dopamine deficiencies in their brains, which were readily correctable with Thorazine or any other major tranquilizer. I discovered that all of the "demons" I was seeing were allergic to Thorazine and that, in nearly every case, a week or two on Thorazine made the "demons" go away and brought the patient closer to his real conflicts. These demons were merely auditory hallucinations. To save self-esteem, these patients were unconsciously amplifying their own unwanted thoughts so loud they seemed like real voices. They felt less guilty when they could convince themselves that these thoughts were coming from some external source ("demons"), rather than from within themselves.

Don't get me wrong, I am a strict biblicist who believes in the inerrancy of Scripture. I believe demons really do exist because the Bible says they do. I believe that there probably are some demon-possessed persons in various parts of the world.

However, I believe Satan is primarily attacking humans in much more subtle ways, as illustrated by C. S. Lewis in his book *The Screwtape Letters*. C. S. Lewis implies in his writings that Satan tends to use the two extremes of complacency and fear to accomplish his purposes rather than intimidating people through supernatural, sensational phenomena such as demon possession.

Biblically, a Christian *cannot* be possessed (controlled) by Satan or any other demon. The Bible tells me, "Stronger is He that is within you [the Holy Spirit] than he that is in the world [Satan]." The Bible also tells me "Resist the devil and he will *flee from you.*" In 1 Corinthians 10:13, the Apostle Paul tells us that as Christians, we are *never* tempted more than we are able to withstand, and that God *always* provides a way to escape each temptation. This verse alone would rule out the possibility of any true believer being demon possesed. However, God's Word warns believers in a number of places (*see,* 1 Peter 5) to watch out for *influences* of demons. Satan has studied human behavior patterns in more depth than any psychiatrist who ever lived. He knows when a human is showing signs of insecurity, and he knows individual human weaknesses, although I doubt that he can read our thoughts. When a human shows false pride to compensate for unconscious inferiority feelings, for example, Satan will tend to use temptations involving lust of the flesh (e.g. sexual fantasies or affairs), lust of the eyes (e.g. materialism), or the pride of life (e.g., power struggles) to compensate for our insecurities (*see* 1 John 2:15, 17).

Thus, psychological and spiritual conflicts become almost indistinguishable in most cases. They are intermeshed together. Satan uses our psychological weaknesses (such as a self-critical attitude in the obsessive-compulsive workaholic) to entice us to sin and render us inefficient to furthering the cause of Christ.

In the demon-possession case in the Bible, all of the afflicted persons were non-Christians and only *one* (the demoniac of Gadarene) had any mental illness. The rest all had physical symptoms (e.g., epilepsy, muteness, and so forth). None of the demon-possessed persons were shaken physically by the disciples the way "demon-possessed" persons get shaken in charismatic services or in sensational movies like the *Exorcist*. Prayer was all that was needed. The missionaries I have talked to who have seen cases of apparent demon possession also used the simple prayer of faith for deliverance. I pray that all of my Christian and non-Christian patients will become free from any influences (including parents as well as demons) that keep them from knowing Christ and from growing toward a more responsible maturity level.

If a person believes he is demon possessed, he usually wants very strongly (on an unconscious level) to believe that he is, no matter how hard he claims to want deliverance. Trying to persuade a delusional person that he is wrong is like squeezing blood out of a turnip. I usually listen to such a patient, showing him respect, while politely letting him know that I doubt demon possession in his case. I try to convince him to take Thorazine or some other major tranquilizer (so I can restore his dopamine level back to normal). Then I am just polite with him and leave him in his delusions until he has taken enough Thorazine for enough days to make his "demons" and other delusions go away automatically. That is when good counseling can really begin.

I usually won't even allow delusional patients to read their Bibles while still delusional, because I am afraid they will misapply Scripture. I have known delusional patients who have read "if your eye offends you, pluck it out" in the Bible and have actually plucked their eyes out, or cut off their sexual organs, and so forth. When they come back to reality through medication, however, the Bible can become a real healing tool in their lives if it is applied the way God intended it to be applied.

I had one delusional patient in his thirties who had lost touch with reality. He was brilliant, with a master's degree in business. He was an air force jet pilot. He had been a Christian for many years and was thoroughly convinced that the Bible was true. When he had a psychotic break, he heard "demon" voices as well as "God's voice," telling him certain things.

A pastor in town, who knew this patient, did not believe me when I told him that confronting this patient with Scripture would probably not do any good while the patient remained delusional. So I allowed the pastor, under my direct supervision, to give it a try. He used excellent biblical arguments to disprove the patient's faulty belief systems. "God's voice" had been telling the patient things which obviously contradicted Scripture. The pastor finally convinced the psychotic pilot that the Bible contradicted his "voices." Do you think this made him give up his voices? Absolutely not! Instead, he gave up his belief in the Bible, since the Bible disagreed with what *he* believed. After several weeks on antipsychotic medication, however, the voices eventually disappeared.

One of the primary areas of study psychiatrists go through is a study of human defense mechanisms. In a book I coauthored (*Comprehensive Textbook of Christian Psychology*, Baker Book House, 1981), I define and give examples of forty defense mechanisms, which are all ways we humans deceive ourselves daily. We humans are so self-deceiving that we would sin daily even if there were no demonic influences in the world (*see* James 1). I am convinced that Satan uses our own individual defense mechanisms (such as rationalization, projection, denial, and repression) to keep us from an awareness of the truth, which would set us free. Through these complex processes, he keeps non-Christians from believing the obvious truth about Christ and keeps Christians less efficient than they could be in serving Christ. Several months of insight-oriented therapy with a trained Christian professional is one of the best paths there is for sure and sound healing.

Paul Meier, M.D.

POWERS AND CHARACTERISTICS OF DEMONS

Demons inflict sickness	Job 2:5-10;Matthew 9:32, 33; 12:22, 23; Luke 9:37-42; 13:11-13
Demons influence people to immoral acts	Matthew 12:43–45; Mark 1:23–27; 5:2–? Luke 4:33–36; 6:18; 8:29; Acts 5:16; 8:7
Demons possess human beings and animals	Matthew 4:24; Mark 5:8–14; Luke 8:2; Acts 8:7; 16:16
Demons can cause mental disorders	Mark 5:1-14
Demons oppose God's children	Matthew 12:45; Ephesians 6:12
Demons communicate false doctrine	1 Kings 22:21–23; 2 Thessalonians 2:2; 1 Timothy 4:1
Demons have supernatural powers	2 Thessalonians 2:9; Revelation 16:14
Demons testify to the divinity of Jesus	Matthew 8:29; Mark 1:23, 24; 3:11; 5:7; Luke 8:28; Acts 19:15
God can use them as he wants	Judges 9:23; 1 Samuel 16:14;
Demons believe and tremble because of God	James 2:19
Demons are to be judged at the general judgment	Matthew 8:29; 2 Peter 2:4; Jude 6
Kill and devour	John 8:44; 1 Peter 5:8
Accuse	Revelation 12:9, 10
Rob	Matthew 13:19

*Consult section on Powers of Angels on pp. 177-84 as demons possess same power as angels, although their characteristics differ. This is because demons are fallen angels.

SATAN'S NAMES

Lucifer (It means "lightbearer," "morning star")	Isaiah 14:12
Satan (It can mean "adversary")	1 Chronicles 21:1; Job 1:6; Zechariah 3:1 Matthew 4:10; 2 Corinthians 2:11 1 Timothy 1:20
Devil (It can mean "slanderer")	Matthew 13:39; John 13:2; Ephesians 6:11 James 4:7
Accuser of the brethren	Revelation 12:10
Dragon, a serpent or a sea creature	Isaiah 51:9; Revelation 12:3, 7; 13:2; 20:2
Beelzebub	Matthew 10:25; 12:24, 27; Mark 3:22
Wicked one or evil one	Matthew 13:19, 38; Ephesians 6:16 1 John 2:13, 14; 5:18
Tempter	Matthew 4:3; 1 Thessalonians 3:5
God of this world	2 Corinthians 4:4
Prince of the power of the air	Ephesians 2:2
Ruler of the evil angels	Matthew 25:41
Prince of devils	Matthew 12:24
Prince of this world	John 12:31; 14:30; 16:11
Serpent	Genesis 3:1; Revelation 12:9

SATAN'S GOAL

This is to fight against God and Man   Genesis 3:17; Job 1:9; 2:4; 1 Peter 5:8

SATAN'S METHODS

He will: Lie   John 8:44; 2 Corinthians 11:3
           Tempt   Matthew 4:1
           Hinder   Zechariah 3:1; 1 Thessalonians 2:18;
                                            Ephesians 6:12
           Sift   Luke 22:31
           Imitate   2 Corinthians 11:14, 15
           Sickness   Luke 13:16; 1 Corinthians 5:5
           Possess   John 13:27

ANGELS

As with demons, the attitude of most people concerning angels is one of disbelief or a "What difference does it make?" perspective. "And if they are good, why be concerned?" Rod Serling, on several occasions used angel characters in his famous television series "The Twilight Zone." They were usually portrayed as jovial and mild-mannered persons whose chief pursuit was accomplishing good deeds. Many parents tell their young children that each one has a guardian angel to protect them, even if the parent doesn't believe it to be true. For many, the reality of angels falls into a fantasy mold. The Bible presents a radically different picture of these divinely created beings.

ANGELS IN HISTORY

The Bible speaks more about angels than any other book found in ancient history. If we look in history, we may find small references to "familiar spirits" in Plato's writings on Socrates or in some Egyptian sources, but these references are always in the context of spiritism and involve ancient mystic religions. Move closer to the Bible and a clearer picture begins to emerge. The religons of Islam and Judaism contain extensive references to angels and their role in the affairs of men. The reason for the abundance of material on angels in these religions is the shared heritage that the Islamic, Jewish and Christian faiths have in the Bible. Neither angels nor man have always been in existence, the Scriptures tell us. Angels and men were both created by the hand of God (Colossians 1:16). As creations of God, they also reflect His image, which is evidenced by the intellect, emotions, and will. While there are a great many differences between angels and humans there are also a lot of similarities.

THEIR ROLE IN OUR LIVES

The Old Testament illustrates a unique relationship between the angels and God. It tells of their presence with God before the creation of the world, their involvement with man in the Garden of

Eden, and their aid in the preservation of the nation of Israel. The Old Testament also states that angels frequently functioned as heavenly messengers. At times these messengers brought good news such as God telling Sarah and Abraham that they would bear a son (Genesis 18:9–12). At other times, the news would be of judgment, as in the case when the two angels visited Lot and told him of the coming destruction of Sodom (Genesis 19). But in all cases, it is an example of a supernatural event in a person's life to receive a message from the Lord via one of these messengers. Many times these messengers were not recognized as angels but seen as strangers and mere mortals.

The primary function of angels in the New Testament is the protection and assistance given to the "heirs of salvation," those who accepted Christ as the Messiah. Angels were involved in the ministry and life of Jesus. They foretold His birth and ministered to Him prior to His death. At the Battle of Armageddon, angels will do battle for Christ when He returns to reign on earth from Jerusalem for one thousand years. In the New Testament, angels are in the position of carrying out orders that will fulfill God's plan for the redemption of the world.

ANGEL OF THE LORD: A SPECIAL CASE

One angel who is set apart from all others is the Angel of the Lord. Throughout the Bible, he plays an enormous role in people's lives. Who is he? Where did he come from, and why is he so important? The Angel of the Lord is found in many places in the Old Testament. He is found with Moses at the burning bush. He guarded the space between the people of Israel and the Egyptians. He is found going before the nation of Israel in the wilderness. He is able to make a contract with the people of Israel that will never be broken. He has the ability to prophesy. He knows about everything in the earth and is known as the redeeming angel. The most important characteristic of the Angel of the Lord is that he received worship.

In the Scriptures, angels are always shown refusing the admiration and worship of men. This is because the worship of angels is forbidden by the laws of Moses. The only two cases where an angel accepts worship are in the cases of Satan and the Angel of the Lord. As a result, Satan was damned, and the Angel of the Lord was not. Why is there this difference? It is because of what Bible scholars call a *theophany*, a supernatural, preincarnate appearance of Christ on earth before His birth. Bible scholars recognize that the Angel of the Lord is one of the most amazing examples found in the Scriptures. No one but God Himself has the power to do the things that the Angel of the Lord did in the Old Testament. To make any other consideration for the Angel of the Lord would be inconsistent with the teaching of the Scripture about the nature of God. The Angel of the Lord is a uniquely different angel.

NATURE OF ANGELS

The impact of angels in the lives of men is determined by their nature, strength, and the will of God. Angels, whenever they appear to man, were always treated with respect, if not awe. In order to understand the effect angels can have on people, one must understand their power and nature.

The Scriptures teach that angels were created by God before the earth was formed. They were created as a company, not as a race and therefore do not procreate. Angels are incorporeal, immortal, and innumerable. This means that the angels cannot be numbered, they possess spiritual bodies, and they can never die. These facts are important when it is realized that angels have been able to watch the progress of man on earth since the beginning. The knowledge and power that they have is far greater than that of man. The accounts of their various appearances on earth have shown them capable of great feats of strength, whether it is slaying over 180,000 men in an evening, or setting men free from prison (2 Kings 19:35; Acts 12).

In light of the knowledge that angels have about men, they are extremely curious about God's plan for imperfect men and women one day ruling over them.

POWERS OF ANGELS

The power of God is unlimited. The power of angels compared to God's power is small, but man's power next to the angels is miniscule. Though the power of angels may be great, their capacity for doing certain tasks is limited. They must move spatially and can encounter delay.

When Daniel the prophet prayed and fasted, requesting guidance from the Lord, an angel appeared to him and told Daniel that he was delayed for twenty-one days due to a confrontation with what is believed to be another fallen angel, Satan (Daniel 10:11–13). Thus, even angels with their great strength may need to summon help as did the angel that came to Daniel. The angel in this verse summoned the archangel Michael.

The fact that the angel needed help and was delayed may seem to be a contradiction of angels' perfect nature, but it is not. One may invent and perfect an engine for a Volkswagen that is the quintessence of perfection. Although it is perfect for the task of motivating a Volkswagen, it will not effectively move an eighteen-wheel tractor-trailer rig. So it is with angels. Some are more powerful than others. The logical question to ask is why? This is not known and cannot be answered. The Scriptures are plain, however, in stating the awesome power of angels.

In attempting to comprehend the impact that this power has on men, let us look at what happened to two people in the Bible when angels appeared to them. When an angel appeared to Mary, the mother of Jesus, she was afraid but was still able to accept the message that was brought to her (Luke 1:26–38). Zacharias, the father of John the Baptist, was great in fear but was still able to carry on a conversation with the angel (Luke 1:8–20). This brings forth the important point that even though we may be shocked by the appearance of the Lord's angels because of a confrontation with a perfectly created being, it is never a paralyzing fear but one of respect for the power that is present. The shepherds were afraid when the angels heralded the birth of Christ, but they were still able to marvel at the message of the angels (Luke 2:8–18). The only time the Scriptures record a fear for one's very life is when the person or persons confronted were opposed to God. A case in point is when the angels appeared at the tomb of Christ to roll away the stone, and a guard unit fell as if they were dead (Matthew 28:4). The guards were trained to know that to lose one's footing and composure while faced with an adversary meant death, yet the guard unit still fell over as though they had been struck dead. The power of angels is a mighty thing for a man to be up against. When that power is working for man, however, the power can be just as awesome from a positive standpoint.

THE MIRACULOUS FLIGHT OF ELDON HILL

In 1945 towards the end of World War II, a flight instructor for the navy experienced what I consider one of the most credible encounters with a supernatural element. Lt. Eldon Hill, prior to his incredible flight, had earned the highest instrument-flight rating given by the navy. Having had four thousand hours of flight time for the navy, Eldon was considered one of the better instructors and check pilots in the national air base, Cuddihy Field, in Corpus Christi, Texas. His training flights in his SNJ trainer plane were done on a daily basis. After a cadet had completed his training assignment, he was then graduated and assigned to a fighter squadron, usually aboard an aircraft carrier. Therefore, the navy carefully screened its instructor pilots.

Eldon was personally interviewed by myself on several occasions to make sure his story checked out. His character is one of undisputed integrity, and he is well thought of in the business community where he lives. My first contact with Eldon was in a business context. I came to seek his services in manufacturing some plastic parts for a new trick I had invented and wanted to market. His straightforward, no-nonsense business acumen was what particularly impressed me. It was through an unusual chain of events that Eldon shared this story with me four years ago. He rarely tells this story because of the almost unbelievable events that occurred. What follows is his story from taped interviews.

UNUSUAL MOVEMENT OF AIR CURRENT (JET STREAM)

I was instructing a cadet in instrument flying at Cuddihy Field, Corpus Christi Naval Air Station. We were flying at an altitude of about 8000 feet in order to be above a broken cloud layer that was a usual condition for the Corpus Christi area. After flying for a while, I noted that my radio was malfunctioning, and I could not communicate with the base tower. My instruments were functioning properly as far as physically flying the aircraft, and because I knew the Corpus Christi area so well, having taught this area for two years, I was not concerned enough to return to base. I was instructing the cadet in using gyro instruments so the radio was not required in order to complete the training session.

While instructing the cadet in the cockpit in front of me, I noticed the cloud layer has closed in solid underneath us, but I assumed the layer was only a thousand feet or so thick as it usually was. Under normal conditions we would descend through the cloud layer on instruments until we dropped underneath on visible contact, at which time we could check known landmarks and know which direction to fly to return to our base.

What I did not know was that the weather conditions had deteriorated and the clouds had formed solid to within 300 feet of the ground. All aircraft had been recalled to base by radio before this deterioration occurred, but since our radio was out, we had not heard the recall.

I also did not know, but was soon to find out, that a rare wind condition had been steadily blowing our aircraft east, out over the Gulf of Mexico, at a high rate of speed. Since the clouds moved at the speed of the wind, we were unaware we were being blown out over water. At the completion of our instruction period, I started descending through this cloud layer, expecting to drop beneath at six or seven thousand feet. When I reached 3000 feet and had not gotten beneath the clouds, I began descending at a more gradual rate. At 1000 feet I was becoming more worried and at 500 feet, very concerned since we had not gotten beneath the clouds. I descended 25 feet at a time until I finally could see water beneath me at 350 feet. Being over water in the Corpus Christi area meant we were east of land, and as every instructor would have done I took a heading of 270° or due west to bring me back to land, hoping that I would then recognize some landmark so I would know whether I was southeast or northeast of my base. I was very concerned at this point because at this low altitude it is very difficult to find any landmarks to identify.

By this time we had flown over an hour on the instruction work and since our aircraft only had a flying supply of gasoline for two hours maximum, this left us a little less than 45 minutes to find an airport to land safely.

I kept telling the cadet that everything was all right and that we would see land soon, trying to keep him from becoming frightened. Since we had not intended flying over water, we were not equipped with Mae Wests, inflatable vests. Therefore, the thought of having to ditch the plane in the water was not something we wanted to do, especially since our radio was out and we could not even advise the radio tower that we were going down in the water. If this had happened, we most likely would have drowned before help could have reached us. I flew the aircraft due west for at least thirty minutes and still had not reached land. I was experiencing disbelief in my instruments, but our training was *never* to doubt your instruments and fly by instinct, so I kept on my due-west course. I had become more and more concerned and even was becoming very frightened, because I knew we only had about fifteen minutes of flying time left before we ran out of gas. We had to reach land soon or it would be too late.

I had attended church during my growing up, and I believed in God in a lukewarm manner, but I had never been strong in my conviction. At this point I felt unless we received help we would die, and I began to pray to God for His help, asking Him to help me get the aircraft in safely. I remember I was more concerned for the young student than I was for myself, because he was in my hands and I was determined to save him. For the next few minutes, I prayed continually and earnestly that the Lord would help us find a place to land safely. At about this time, my engine sputtered, as we had drained the right-wing tank of gasoline. I quickly switched to the left tank and hit my booster pump, and the engine started running smoothly again. I knew I now had maybe five to ten minutes flying time left in the left tank, and then we would go down into the water. I again prayed for help saying, "Lord, it's out of my hands; I can't do anything else; it's in Your hands to do Your will." I felt nothing for a minute or two and then I felt a slight chill run up my back and a warm glow coming over me slowly. As this warmth increased, I became relaxed and calm and began to have a feeling that everything was all right. I did not hear a word spoken, see anyone, or physically feel anyone touch me. But the warmth filling the cockpit of the aircraft and a feeling that the Lord was standing behind me with His hands slightly above, but not touching my shoulders, made me feel that I was handling the controls of the aircraft, but that I was being guided and directed.

Ahead I could barely make out the coastline. My normal training in a situation like this would have been to turn the aircraft and fly parallel to the beach 200 or 300 yards offshore, ditch the aircraft, and swim ashore, but I did not even consider this because I had complete confidence that the Lord was directing me to fly on over the beach, which I did. I felt I was to make a smooth but sharp turn to the left and without looking left I started my turn, putting my wheels and flaps down as we were making the turn. Right in front of me as I straightened out, was a straight short strip of land with some sparse grass growing on what appeared to have been at one time a road. I was completely relaxed and confident as we settled in for a landing, rolled to the short end and stopped. As soon as we stopped, I reached forward, turned off the switch to the engine and suddenly, like turning off an electric light, the warm-glow feeling over my body and throughout the cockpit was gone. I slid the hood back, leaned forward, and emotionally thanked God for getting us down safely and helping me save the life of the cadet.

When we climbed out of the aircraft, the cadet spoke to me, saying, "Sir; that was really a close call, wasn't it?" He said he was so frightened, he prayed for the Lord to help us get down safely, and just before we saw the beach he had felt a warmth and a presence in the cockpit and knew we would be all right. I told the cadet we had experienced something that few people experience, and that we owed our lives to the Lord. I asked the cadet when this feeling went away, and he said it was at about the time we stopped the plane and slid the hood open. Without communication between us, we had had the same experiences at precisely the same time.

After sitting for some fifteen minutes discussing our emotional experience we decided to try to walk for help so we could call the naval base and let them know we were safe. We were now overdue by over an hour. After walking west for a few minutes, following what appeared to be an old rutted road, we came out on a farm-to-market road and observed an old, dilapidated pickup truck coming toward us. The truck stopped and an old man asked if we needed help. We told him we had had a forced landing, did not know where we were, and would appreciate it if he could take us to the nearest telephone. He said there was a small outlying field, used for practice landings by the Victorio Army Air Corps, not too many miles away and that he could take us there. When we arrived at the army practice field, we found they had gasoline in fifty-five-gallon drums and could give us whatever we needed to refuel our plane and fly back to Corpus Christi. We found we had been blown so far east and north that we had come ashore on the coast south of Freeport, Texas. I telephoned and advised our base we were down but okay, would refuel and fly the plane out and on to base. The farmer helped load a drum of gasoline, drove us back to our aircraft, helped us refuel, and said he would take the empty drum back to the field. We thanked the farmer for his assistance and offered to pay him, but he would accept no pay. I asked him again for his name, and he gave it to me and told me that he lived in a small rural town. He moved his truck some distance away, and we started the plane and returned to Corpus without any further trouble.

For some reason, neither the cadet nor myself, on landing, told anyone of this emotional experience, saying only that we were blown offshore and ran out of gas. I suppose we were afraid no one would believe what happened.

The next day was Saturday, and I had no instruction flights. And because I was still so overcome with this emotional experience, I checked out a plane and flew by myself to find the strip we had landed on and to look at all the surrounding terrain. I found the army practice field, the farm-to-market road, and the turnoff to the old road we had walked on, but to my shock I could not find the strip we had landed on. I flew back and forth searching for this strip for half an hour before giving up. It just wasn't there; it apparently had disappeared. Until this time I knew the Lord had gotten us down safely, but I did not realize he had placed the strip there for just long enough for us to land on and to later take off from. Several times later both the cadet and I tried to find the strip, but to no avail.

Several weeks later I tried to reach the old man to thank him again for his help, but I had misplaced his route number. So I called the post office in the little town, talked to the postmaster, and was told he knew everyone in town, had never heard of the name I gave him, and was sure no one by that name had a rural box in his area.

I do not know whether this old man just happened along, or if he also was put there by the Lord to help us through our experience. I am sure, however, that the Lord heard our prayers, that His presence was with us in the aircraft, and that He caused us to land safely. I would not be alive today had the Lord not helped us.

Several years later, I was talking to a psychologist friend of mine and told him of this experience. He explained that he believes we all possess an inner power enabling us to accomplish phenomenal things, and that I had apparently been able to harness that power that had remained untapped before. I told him this could not be the answer because there was no way I could have found the strip at the same time I was out of gas. And his solution did not explain how both the cadet and I experienced the same things at precisely the same time without communicating with each other until after the experience.

Thirty-five years have passed since this experience, and many times I've prayed for the Lord to help me when loved ones have been sick or when family members needed help, or when there have been business problems. I am sure some of my prayers have been answered, but never before that day in 1945 or since have I felt the warm glow and the presence of the Lord and the feeling of knowing He was with me as He was on that day.

Eldon Hill

POWERS AND CHARACTERISTICS OF ANGELS

Theophany (Angel of the Lord):

1. The Angel of the Lord — Exodus 3:2

2. The Angel of God — Exodus 14:19

3. My Angel — Exodus 32:34

4. The Angel of the Lord — Judges 2:1

5. The Angel of the Lord — Judges 13:6

6. An Angel of God — 2 Samuel 14:17–20

7. The Angel of His Presence — Isaiah 63:9

What Angels Are Called (Other Than Angel):

8. Angel of the Lord — Matthew 1:20; 24; 2:13; 19; 28:2
Luke 1:11
Acts 5:19; 8:26; 12:7; 23

9. Morning Stars — Job 38:7

10. Hosts — Genesis 2:1; 32:2
Joshua 5:14
Deuteronomy 4:19; 17:3
1 Kings 22:19
1 Chronicles 12:22
Psalms 33:6; 103:21; 148:2
Luke 2:13
Nehemiah 9:6

11. Rulers-Authorities	Ephesians 3:10
	Colossians 1:16
12. Sons of God	Genesis 6:2; 4
	Job 1:6; 2:1; 38:7
13. Ministering Spirits	Hebrews 1:14

Nature of Angels

14. They are created	Genesis 2:1
	Psalms 148:2; 5
	Nehemiah 9:6
	Colossians 1:16
	John 1:3
15. Before the earth was	Job 38:7; 4–7
16. To give glory to God	Psalms 148:2; 5
	Isaiah 6:1–3
17. Holy	Genesis 1:31; 2:3
	Matthew 25:31
	Mark 8:38
18. As a company they do not procreate	Matthew 22:28–30
19. Incorporeal	Psalms 104:4
	Hebrews 1:7; 14

20. Innumerable	Deuteronomy 33:2 (10,000 in this verse literally translated "myriads")
	2 Kings 6:17
	Job 25:3
	Psalms 68:17
	Daniel 7:10
	Matthew 26:53
	Hebrews 12:22
	Jude 1:14
21. Immortal, they do not die	Luke 20:36
22. Angels are ministers (God's servants)	Hebrews 1:7
23. Angels are messengers of God	Psalms 103:20

Powers and Capabilities of Angels

24. Angels are responsible to God	Ezekiel 28:12–19
	Matthew 25:41
	John 16:11
	Psalms 103:20, 21
25. Angels guard the way to the tree of life.	Genesis 3:24

26. Law given by angels

Acts 7:53
Galatians 3:19
Hebrews 2:2
Daniel 4:13–17; 8:15–26
9:21–27; 10:10–20
Zechariah 1:19–21
Acts 8:26
Galatians 3:19
Hebrews 2:2
2 Kings 1:15

27. Relay messages (to prophets
and others)

Revelation 1:1; 5:2–14;
7:1–3; 7:11–17;
8:2–13; 22:6–16

28. This means angels have the
power of communication

Revelation 5:6; 7:1-3;
12:10–12

29. Angels have the power of
speech (see verses on relaying
messages to the prophets)

Matthew 28:5
John 20:12, 13

Other examples, they
announced the birth of:
Sampson
John the Baptist
Jesus

Judges 13
Luke 1:11–20
Matthew 1:20, 21
Luke 1:28–38; 2:9–15

30. Angels must move spatially

Daniel 9:21–23

31. They can get delayed

Daniel 10:10–14

32. Angels are greater in
    strength than man

Matthew 28:2; Mark 16:3, 4
Psalms 103:20; 2 Peter 2:11
                    (in context)
2 Thessalonians 1:7

33. Angels have wisdom
    (Satan's was corrupted)

Ezekiel 28:17

34. Angels have limited authority
    (Satan had authority that
    God gave him)

Psalms 91:11, 12; Romans 8:38
Colossians 1:16; Revelation 7:2

35. Angels have control over
    elements or objects

Job 1:12; 2:6
Acts 12:5–11; Revelation 7:1; 16:8

36. Angels watch us

1 Corinthians 4:9; Daniel 4:13–17

37. Angels can get tired and
    need help (Gabriel needed
    help from Michael which shows
    their strength is not unlimited)

Revelation 12:7–8; Daniel 10:13

38. Angels can perceive the purpose
    of men

Matthew 28:5

39. Angels protect God's people   Hebrews 1:14; Genesis 19:10–16
                                        Daniel 3:28; Acts 12:7–11
                                        Psalms 91:1, 11–12

40. Angels can provide man's   Genesis 21:17–20; Psalms 78:23–25
    physical needs   1 Kings 19:5–7; Matthew 4:11
41. Angels can eat as men   Genesis 18:8; 19:3; Psalms 78:24–25

42. Angels have the ability to   Luke 1:11–13; 26–29
    appear subject only to the   Luke 2:9; Acts 5:19
    will of God

43. Angels can appear in dreams   Matthew 1:20

44. Angels can appear to   Daniel 8:15–17; Matthew 28:1–7
    natural sight   Genesis 18:19;
                                       Matthew 1:20; Luke 1:26
                                       John 20:12; Hebrews 13:2

45. Their identity is not always   Jude 6
    known so they can be   Hebrews 13:2; Genesis 18:2; 19:1–8
    mistaken for mere men

46. Angels may appear in the   Daniel 10:5, 6; 7:9
    form of an unusual man   Matthew 28:3; Acts 1:10

47. When angels appear they have
    various effects on men:
    Joseph was not affected   Matthew 1:18–25
    Mental Anguish came to Mary   Luke 1:29, 34, 38
    Zacharias had fear   Luke 1:12
    Shepherds were afraid   Luke 2:9, 15, 18
    Loss of composure and physical   Matthew 28:4
    strength came to the Roman
    guard

48. Animals can sometimes see angels

Numbers 22: 26-28, 31

49. Angels are agents in answering prayer

Daniel 9:20-24; 10:12
Ezekiel 30:1-10; Acts 12:1-17
Revelation 8:2-4

50. Angels strengthen and encourage

Luke 22:43; Acts 5:19-20

51. One angel will bind Satan for 1,000 years

Revelation 20:1-3

52. Angels battle other angels

Daniel 10:13; Revelation 12:7-8

53. Angels command other angels

Revelation 7:1-3,14:17,18

54. Angels are part of God's army

Psalms 89:6, 8

55. Many angels can be in a small space (a legion is equal to 6,000 troops)

Luke 8:30

56. Angels may appear in any number

Genesis 18:1,2; Luke 1:26-29
Luke 2:13; John 20:12;
Acts 1:10

57. Angels will gather believers at Christ's return

Matthew 24:30; 31 13:40 ,41
1 Thessalonians 4:16

58. Angels are used by God to exclude (set out) human wickedness

Genesis 18:22; 19:1; 10, 11

59. God's angels execute judg-
    ment on God's enemies   Acts 12:23 2 Kings 19:35

60. God's angels execute judg-
    ment on men   2 Samuel 24:13–16
    (study also Revelation and
    angels being used in bowl and
    trumpet judgments)

61. All angels knew God and were
    commanded to praise Him   Psalms 148:1, 2, 5; 103:20, 21

62. Angels enjoy God's presence   Matthew 18:10; Job 38:4–7

63. Angels are curious about
    salvation   1 Peter 1:11, 12

64. Angels worship God   Isaiah 6:1–4; Revelation 5:11–14

65. Angels rejoice when a sinner
    is saved   Luke 15:10

66. Angels do not know that exact
    time of Christ's return but
    will participate in it.   Matthew 24:36; Mark 13:32

67. Angels can be aware of future
    events and men's prayers when
    informed by God   Daniel 9:20–23; Luke 1:13–16

68. Recognize the deity of Christ   Revelation 5:11–14

69. Angels attend the death of   Luke 16:22; Jude 9
    the righteous   Daniel 12: 1–3

PSYCHIATRIC COMMENTS ON ANGELS

I have heard a number of stories similar to Eldon Hill's from reputable persons of good emotional stability. I believe some of these stories, including Mr. Hill's, are true. When a person tells me a story like Mr. Hill's, I assume that the person is (1) lying to get attention; (2) delusional; or (3) telling the truth, in that order. Some of the more believable angel stories I have heard, have been told to me in private by acquaintances who admitted that they were afraid to tell me because I might think they were crazy.

A skeptic could postulate that the warm sensation felt by both Mr. Hill and the cadet simultaneously may have been a physiological response to stress involving the dilation of small blood vessels in the skin. However, the fact that the small strip on which they landed disappeared and could not be found by either Hill or the cadet, even though both knew the exact location of the strip relative to the army airfield, is nearly impossible to explain away.

The Bible does tell Christians that some of us have "entertained angels unawares." This means that a number of Christians have had helpful interactions with angels without even knowing that the human form was really an angel. Hebrews 1 tells us we each have a guardian angel, which is certainly reassuring.

Paul Meier, M.D.

CONCLUSION

I made the point in the introduction to this section of the text that it was exceedingly difficult to prove scientifically the reality of demons and angels. To prove via scientific means involves only an engaging of one's mind and this is where the dilemma begins. Man cannot perfectly perceive things of a spiritual nature with a finite mind. One can only perceive things of the spirit with the spirit. One can understand the validity of biblical prophecy as it involves an intellectual course of action. The Lord created us with a mind and He expects us to use it. He also created us, however, with a spirit, and we are expected to use it too. For some, the idea of a spirit seems absurd, while to those who experience growth in the spirit which the Lord created in each of us, it is more real than the physical growth of the mind or body. The reason lies in the fact that the body will die, but the spirit is eternal, and thus growth of the spirit has a deeper sense of permanence than growth of the mind or body. For Christians it is an easy thing to come to grips with the fact that there are two sources of supernatural power in the universe—that of the Lord and that of Satan. Both the Lord and Satan are appealing to our spirits but in different ways; one for good and one for evil.

Eldon Hill's unusually credible story is an example of the Lord interceding in his life to affect a change as well as save his life. Many stories such as the one detailed by Eldon have been told and printed. To be sure, many were probably not the result of the intervention of a supernatural agent. Was it an angel that picked up Eldon and the young cadet? There can be no positive proof. I believe that the old man was an angel, but again I can't prove it scientifically. One thing is certain. The open strip of land on which Eldon landed vanished.

In 2 Kings 6 (vv. 16, 17 NAS) the writer records the story of an invasion of Israel by Syria. Elisha, the prophet, was asked by his panicked servant what they were to do as they were surrounded by horses and chariots. Elisha then said:

> "Do not fear, for those who are with us are more than those who are with them." Then Elisha prayed and said, "O, Lord, I pray, open his eyes that he may see." And the Lord opened the servant's eyes, and he saw; and behold, the mountain was full of horses and chariots of fire all around Elisha.

The servant beheld the angels of the Lord in the hills surrounding the Syrian army. Elisha did not pray for the servant to see the angels through his fleshly eyes but rather through his spiritual eyes—his spirit. Jesus made it clear many times throughout His ministry that one can only perceive things of the spirit with the spirit. The trouble begins when we try to perceive things of the spirit with the mind.

Pseudo-occultic phenomena have been shown to be that which is brought about by that which is physical or psychological. There is no need to fear them other than in the danger of furthering superstition.

Many Christians think that fire walking is satanic. They are correct, and they are at the same time incorrect. It is satanic in the sense that Satan can use it to further superstition, which will draw people away from the Lord. It is not satanic in the sense of a direct intervention of a supernatural power that enables one to walk across a bed of hot coals. We must perceive things of the spirit with the spirit and that of the physical or psychological with the mind. The same rule applies to those of a non-Christian mind-set. If they are to come to grips with the claims of Christ, the reality of angels, and so forth, they must use the spirit. This is not a religious statement but an axiom of understanding that is as real as the law of gravity.

We have made it clear that one need have no fear of the work of Satan and his fallen angels, because through the authority of Christ one can have ultimate power over them and their work. While it is doubtful that many reading this text will ever personally encounter an angel or demon, it is comforting to know that we need not fear them.

It is hoped that those who do not believe in a supernatural element will be pointed in a positive and responsible direction, minus the trappings of mythical concepts. It is not common knowledge, but the one subject Jesus talked about more than any other in His ministry was the kingdom of heaven. Those that seek true and ultimate knowledge and understanding should heed His advice.

> But seek ye first the kingdom of God, and his righteousness; and all these things shall be added unto you.
>
> Matthew 6:33.

SOURCE NOTES

Chapter 2

1. Francis A. Schaeffer, *He Is There and He Is Not Silent* (Wheaton, Ill.: Tyndale House Publishers, 1972), p. 47.
2. Os Guiness, *Encircling Eyes* (Downer's Grove, Ill: Inter-Varsity Press, 1974), p. 17.
3. *Ibid.*, pp. 11-16.
4. Milbourne Christopher, *ESP, Seers and Psychics* (New York: Thomas Y. Crowell Co., 1970), pp. 55, 56.
5. D. H. Rawcliffe, *Occult and Supernatural Phenomena* (New York: Dover Publications Inc., 1959), pp. 394, 395.

Chapter 3

6. *Ibid.*, p. 136.
7. Kurt Koch, *The Devil's Alphabet* (Grand Rapids, Mich.: Kregel Publications, 1969), p. 97.
8. *Ibid.*, p. 32.
9. *Ibid.*, p. 40.
10. Christopher, *op. cit.*, p. 135.

Chapter 4

11. Rawcliffe, *op. cit.*, p. 334.
12. Kurt Koch, *Between Christ and Satan* (Grand Rapids, Mich.: Kregel Publications, 1972), p. 39.
13. Christopher, *op. cit.*, p. 140.

Chapter 5

14. Koch, *Between Christ and Satan*, p. 100.
15. Kurt Koch, *Christian Counselling and Occultism* (Grand Rapids, Mich.: Kregel Publications, 1973), pp. 45, 46.
16. *Ibid.* p. 47.
17. Christopher, *op cit.*, p. 122.

Chapter 6

18. Christopher, *Ibid.*, p. 126.
19. Koch, *Christian Counselling and Occultism*, p. 39.

Chapter 7

20. Koch, *Between Christ and Satan*, p. 103.
21. Rawcliffe, *op. cit.*, pp. 141, 142.

Chapter 8

22. Kurt Koch, *Occult Bondage and Deliverance* (Grand Rapids, Mich.: Kregel Publications, 1970), p. 42.
23. Tim Timmons, *Chains of the Spirit* (Grand Rapids, Mich.: Baker Book House, 1973), p. 25.

Chapter 10

24. Ronald Pearsall, *The Table Rappers* (New York: St. Martin's Press, 1972), p. 29.
25. Christopher, *op cit.*, p. 173.

Chapter 11

26. Ruth Montgomery, *A Gift of Prophecy* (New York: William Morrow & Company, 1965), p. vii.
27. Ruth Montgomery, *A Gift of Prophecy* (New York: Bantam Books, 1970).
28. *Ibid.*
29. Christopher, *op. cit.*, pp. 80, 81.
30. *Ibid.*
31. Frank D. Minirth, M.D. and Paul D. Meier, M.D. *Happiness Is a Choice* (Grand Rapids, Mich.: Baker Book House, 1978), pp. 88, 64.

Chapter 12

32. Carl Sagan, *Broca's Brain* (New York: Random House, 1979), p. 282.
33. *Ibid.*, p. 283.
34. *Ibid.*, p. 310.
35. *Ibid.*, pp. 288, 289.
36. Josh McDowell, *More Than a Carpenter* (Wheaton, Ill.: Tyndale House Publishers, Inc., 1977), p. 37.
37. *The New Encyclopedia Britannica*, Micropedia Vol. VIII, p. 985.
38. McDowell, *op. cit.*, p. 38.

39. *Ibid.*, p. 47.
40. William F. Albright, *Recent Discoveries in Bible Lands* (New York: Funk and Wagnalls, 1955), p. 136.
41. Sir Frederic Kenyon, *The Bible and Archaeology* (New York: Harper and Row, 1940), pp. 288, 289.
42. John W. Montgomery, *History and Christianity* (Downers Grove, Ill., Inter-Varsity Press, 1971), p. 29.
43. McDowell, *op. cit.* pp. 54, 55.
44. Josh McDowell, *Evidence That Demands a Verdict* (Arrowhead Springs, San Bernardino, Calif. Campus Crusade for Christ International, 1972), p. 56.
45. *Ibid.*, p. 58.
46. Robert Dick Wilson, "What Is An Expert?" n.p., *The Bible League Quarterly*, 1955.
47. *Ibid.*
48. *Ibid.*
49. Dr. John Walvoord, *Daniel* (Chicago: Moody Press, 1971), p. 22.
50. Wilson, *op. cit.*
51. William F. Albright, in *Christianity Today*, Vol. 7, Jan. 18, 1963, p. 3.
52. McDowell, *More Than a Carpenter,* pp. 51, 52.
53. Robert Grant, *Historical Introduction to the New Testament* (New York: Harper and Row, 1963), p. 302.
54. Will Durant, "Caesar and Christ," *The Story of Civilization*, Vol. 3 (New York: Simon and Schuster, 1944), p. 557.
55. McDowell, *More Than a Carpenter*, p. 73.
56. *Ibid.*, p. 74.
57. Sir William Ramsay, *The Bearing of Recent Discovery on the Trustworthiness of the New Testament* (London: Hodder and Stoughton Ltd., 1915), p. 222.
58. Norman L. Geisler and William E. Nix, *A General Introduction to the Bible* (Chicago: Moody Press, 1968), p. 366.
59. McDowell, *Evidence That Demands a Verdict*, p. 167.
60. Peter W. Stoner and Robert C. Newman, *Science Speaks* (Chicago: Moody Press, 1976), p. 106.
61. *Ibid.*, p. 112.
62. *Science News*, Vol. 115, June 9, 1979, p. 377.

Chapter 13

63. C. S. Lewis, *The Screwtape Letters* (New York: Macmillan Publishing Co., Inc., 1961), pp. 32, 33.